SO HOT - BOOK 2

so right

USA TODAY BESTSELLING AUTHOR

DARCY BURKE

Copyright

So Right
Copyright © 2017 Darcy Burke
All rights reserved.

ISBN: 1944576142
ISBN-13: 9781944576141

Book design © Darcy Burke.
Cover design © Elizabeth Mackey.
Editing: Linda Ingmanson.

For my dear friends Bonnie and Marty

Over a decade of laughter and memories together—
and here's to many, many more!

Chapter One
❦

Ribbon Ridge, Late September

LUKE WESTCOTT DESCENDED the hillside, his gaze roving over the dark purple fruit hanging among the vines. The volunteer workers had made good progress today, but needed to be back at it again tomorrow. And probably the day after that, since their workforce would decrease dramatically. Today they had every Westcott and Archer in attendance, along with some random guests here and there, plus their hired help.

He could see one of those guests, Kelsey McDade, walking among the pumpkins he'd planted at the base of this slope. He'd met Kelsey on several occasions—she worked at the pub in town and was a friend of his brother's girlfriend—and liked her. Curious as to what she was doing, he continued downward until the ground evened out a bit. "You lost?" he asked.

Her back was to him, and she jumped. Turning, she held her hand to her chest. "You scared me."

He couldn't see her eyes because she was wearing sunglasses. Pity, because he recalled that they were pale blue and quite expressive. "I didn't mean to."

He slipped his sunglasses off and blinked against the brightness of the brilliant sun. It was a picture-perfect fall day with a crisp, cloudless, blue sky and temperatures in the eighties. Sweat trickled down his back as if to remind him how hot it was.

She pushed her glasses up onto her head. She'd pulled her long, dark hair into two braids, which fell against her shoulders. "Am I in trouble? I should probably get back to work."

He chuckled. "You're perfectly entitled to take a break. I really appreciate you coming out today."

"I was thrilled to be invited. I'm sure it sounds odd, but harvesting wine grapes is a cool thing to check off the bucket list."

"That doesn't sound odd to me at all, but then, I'm pretty much a wine grape freak."

She tipped her head to the side. "And how'd that happen?"

"I worked at a local vineyard in high school, and, uh, I liked it a lot." That was a bit of an understatement, but he wouldn't go into boring detail about how he'd become obsessed with nurturing the vines as if they were pets.

She glanced up the hill toward the vineyard. "Well, you seem to be very good at it. Not that I have any idea what I'm talking about, but the fruit looks gorgeous, and I can attest to the wine being delicious."

"You can thank Hayden for that." Hayden Archer was the winemaker and one of the owners of their winery along with Luke and his two brothers, Cameron and Jamie.

"Sure, but he needs good grapes to start with, doesn't he?"

Luke smiled. He wasn't always very adept at accepting praise. "Yes. So what are you doing in the pumpkin patch?"

"Oh!" She looked around at the ripening fruit at her feet. "I love pumpkin patches. This is my absolute favorite time of the year. Apple cider, pumpkin spice everything, Halloween… It's the best."

He nodded, thinking he couldn't agree more. "Who doesn't love fall? Granted, it's my busiest time of the year with the harvest, but that's another reason I love it."

"That's so great you have a job that you love." Her tone held a wistful quality that stirred him.

He took a step toward her. "You don't?"

"I do, actually. At least part-time anyway."

He recalled that she was also the librarian at the new library in town. "Damn, I still haven't stopped in to the library to check things out. My bad. In my defense, it really is my busiest time of the year."

She smiled as she glanced down, her toe nudging a pumpkin vine. "It's no big deal. Stop in whenever."

"I will. I promise." He turned and took a few steps. "I planted white pumpkins too, but they aren't doing quite as well. I'm going to have to do some research." If he wasn't careful, he could see himself becoming as obsessed with the pumpkin vines as he was with the grape. "The goal is to have a pumpkin patch that will entice families to come out for a harvest festival experience—hayrides, pumpkins, and that apple cider you mentioned."

"What, no wine?"

He laughed. "I forgot the most important thing! Yes, wine for the grown-ups. We reel them in with the kiddos and then get them to sign up for our wine club."

She rested her hands on her hips, smiling at him. "Sounds like a foolproof marketing plan."

"Credit Cameron. He's the marketing guru."

Her gaze took on a calculated interest—or so it seemed to him. "You don't like to take credit for stuff, do you?" She'd figured him out pretty quick.

"Well, the marketing stuff is absolutely *not* my forte, but yeah, I guess you could say I like to linger in the background." He didn't mind telling her that. It wasn't a secret or anything.

"I totally get that. The spotlight isn't my thing either."

It was always nice to find a kindred spirit. "So we're two introverts hiding in the pumpkin patch."

She laughed, and the sound seemed to go with the gorgeous day—bright and cheerful, and it made him feel good right down to his soul. "That sounds about right, at least for me."

"Is that why you're picking grapes alone?" he asked. "Most everyone else is with a partner or a group."

"I was with a group earlier. Before lunch. I'd reached maximum companionship." She shrugged. "What can I say, I enjoy my alone time."

Wow. Now his interest was really piqued. One of the primary issues in his last relationship had been his ex's need for constant togetherness. He'd loved her—he thought—but he needed his space. "Me too," he murmured. "But I suppose that means I should leave you to it." He was loath to move, however.

"No, I'm good." A faint blush swathed the elegant sweep of her cheekbones. "Since you're here, I'd like to ask you something."

He edged toward her, suddenly eager. "Anything." *Anything?*

"I'm working on a research project at the library. With Brooke and Crystal."

Brooke was his brother Cameron's girlfriend, although Luke was pretty certain an engagement was imminent. "I've heard Brooke talk about it—the brick we found here, right?"

When they'd demolished the house that had been inhabited by the former vineyard owner, they'd found an interesting brick near the foundation. The letters "BNR" and the year 1879 were engraved in it, and determining its meaning had become a quest for Brooke, Kelsey, and their friend Crystal Donovan.

"Yes. We think it came from the original homestead that was on this property—the initials stand for Bird's Nest Ranch. It was built in 1879. We found a photograph of the house, including the couple who lived here. We're trying to find out more about them. We'd love to find the actual house, or the remains of it, anyway."

This all sounded vaguely familiar to Luke, but he admitted he hadn't paid attention too closely. Because he was busy. Geez, maybe he was a little too focused on his job. He could think of plenty of people who would agree with him. Maybe everyone. "Forgive me, and I hope this doesn't make me sound like an asshat, but why are you all so interested?"

She lifted one shoulder in a slight shrug. "Crystal's a history buff, and I guess Brooke and I are just along for the ride. I think it's fascinating. I've only lived here in Ribbon Ridge a couple of years, but the community is so close-knit and very hometown proud, I thought people would be excited to unearth some history."

He definitely felt like an asshat, especially since those three women—Kelsey and her two pals—weren't even from Ribbon Ridge, whereas he'd been born and raised here. As had his father. And his grandfather had moved here as a young man after graduating from Williver College, which was less than thirty minutes away. Yep, asshat status confirmed. "This sounds like a very cool project, and we're lucky to have you all working on it."

She brightened. "Thanks. I'm looking forward to including it in the historical section of the library."

"Oh?" He didn't have to feign interest, not when she talked about something that made her face light up like the Fourth of July.

"We have some space upstairs at the library that I'm going to use for exhibits. First on the schedule is a Ribbon Ridge retrospective. The county has been very supportive in helping us find documents and artifacts that will be of interest to the community. The Archer family has also been very helpful."

Of course—they were Ribbon Ridge's first family. "I'm surprised none of them are helping."

"Well, they are. I mean, they're providing documents and some of their own historical information and artifacts that belong to their family. Crystal's best friend is Alaina Archer, and she's as involved as she can be."

Given that Alaina was both a famous movie star and expecting her second child, Luke imagined she had her hands full. "She's not even an Archer by birth."

Kelsey smiled. "True. But I have the feeling the family doesn't care. They embrace everyone as if they're part of the family. I've only spent a little bit of time with them, but they've made me feel more welcome and more comfortable than I ever have."

Luke could understand and agree with that. He'd known them his whole life. His older brother, Cameron, had been tight with Hayden since grade school. And his older half brother, Dylan, was married to Sara Archer.

He studied Kelsey, picking up on what she said. "More than you ever have? That makes me curious."

She looked off to the side then, and he had the sense

this was a topic she preferred to avoid. As a fellow introvert, he understood. And would help her out of the awkward corner he'd inadvertently steered her into. "So this research project—what's next?"

When she turned her head toward him again, there was a glint of gratitude in her gaze. Or maybe he just imagined it because that was how he would've felt. "We're searching for the location of the house, starting with looking at maps at the historical society. Then we may hire an archaeological crew to find the actual house. Rather, the foundation."

"So you know the house was here?" He didn't like the idea of anyone digging around his vineyard. These vines were over twenty years old. No way would he let anyone kill them.

At her nod, he continued. "I, uh, I hope you don't plan to tear my vineyard apart."

Her eyes widened in horror. "Oh no, of course not! We wouldn't want to harm your grapes. We don't even know for sure where the house was located. Maybe it isn't even in the vineyard."

That was a possibility—one that he'd cling to. "Even if it is, there may not be much—or anything—to find. When they planted the vines in the early nineties, it's likely they disrupted any archaeological evidence."

Her expression turned to disappointment. "That would be a shame. I'm going to hope that the homestead wasn't in the vineyard."

"Or where any of our buildings are standing," he said, thinking this project could be a real headache. He watched as consternation wrinkled her brow and felt bad for raising doubt and being difficult. He took a step toward her. "I'm sorry, I didn't mean to put a damper on your enthusiasm." Perhaps asshat didn't adequately describe him in this instance. He might've gone full jackass.

"It's okay," she said. "All valid points."

"Sure, but did I really need to be the bearer of bad news? I mean, what the hell do I know about any of this?"

"You're concerned about your vineyard. As you should be." She reached out and briefly touched his sleeve. He wished the contact had been firmer and lasted longer. "I'll keep you posted on everything."

That relieved him, but also ignited a spark. He had a reason to keep in touch with her. Beyond just dropping in on her at the library. He smiled, pleased with this turn of events.

Wait, was he thinking of dating her? He'd been focused on the vineyard since breaking up with Paige. He didn't miss dating, and he wasn't looking for a romantic entanglement of any kind.

Whoa, boy, he cautioned. You're just having a nice conversation with an attractive woman.

His gaze dipped to the tattered hem of her jean shorts and the long shapely legs that descended to her scuffed hiking boots. It was ridiculous, but he found that small detail incredibly alluring. A woman who enjoyed being outside was a woman he wanted to get to know.

He had to amend his earlier assessment—she was a *really* attractive woman.

She cocked her head to the side and narrowed her eyes at him. "What will you do if the foundation is right here in your pumpkin patch?"

He was pretty sure she was teasing him. He blew out a breath as he stuck his fingers in his pockets. "I'm afraid I can't let you dig these vines up either. They're special, you see. These pumpkins are magic."

"As in Cinderella's coach?"

He nodded. "Yep, but listen, you can't tell anyone." He lowered his voice to a whisper. "Those white ones turn into unicorns."

She giggled then. "You're a dork."

He grinned at her, thinking how pretty she was with her pink cheeks and sparkling pale blue eyes that were probably the color of Cinderella's gown. "Unabashedly."

"Hey, Luke!" The call came down the hillside.

Luke turned his head, recognizing his brother Jamie's voice.

"I'll let you go," Kelsey said. "I need to get back to work anyway—before the boss fires me."

Luke fixed her with a steady stare. "He wouldn't dare."

She gave him a saucy smile as she slid her sunglasses back into place and turned. "Good to know."

He watched her walk up the hill to the vineyard, her backside swaying as she ascended. Yeah, hiking with her was now officially on his list. Next time he saw her, he'd ask.

Shit, when? His life was harvest, harvest, and more harvest.

"Were you down here flirting with Kelsey?" Jamie asked, turning his head to look after her departing figure.

"No. We were just chatting. No big deal." Luke put his sunglasses back on.

"Uh-huh." Jamie gave him a teasing smile.

Luke rolled his eyes, not that his little brother could see them. "Did you need something?"

"Just wondered where you got off to," Jamie said. "I

probably should have left you alone. Well, alone with Kelsey."

Luke was used to taking shit from his brothers on a variety of subjects that included his love life. And since he didn't hesitate to dish it out, he was prepared to take it. "It's not like that, but thanks for playing." He started walking up the hill toward the winery. "What, you and Madison are cooling off so it's time to stick your nose in my business?" He slid Jamie a sardonic smirk.

"Ha. There's not much to cool off—as you well know."

This was true. Because Luke shared a house with his brother just outside downtown Ribbon Ridge, they were pretty much up in each other's business. Maybe not 24/7, but certainly more than Luke would like. He preferred his own space, but property was at a premium in Ribbon Ridge. Both he and Jamie had moved back to town about two years ago to start up this winery, and since neither wanted to live with their parents, they'd decided to rent this house together. But Luke was starting to get antsy. He missed having his own digs. He was actually thinking of looking into one of those tiny houses.

"I thought you'd be happy about that," Jamie added. "I didn't think you liked Madison that much."

"Eh, she's all right." She was nice enough, but very high maintenance—the kind of girl who pouted when Jamie wasn't available when she wanted him to be and expected him to change aspects of his personality for her. Now that he thought about it, she wasn't all that different from Paige. At least Paige hadn't been annoying.

Jamie hiked up the hill beside him. "Didn't you call her a soul-sucking banshee or something?"

Luke nodded. "Because she is." Last weekend, she'd demanded Jamie bail on dinner at their parents' house because her plans had been canceled. When Jamie had refused, she'd chewed him out. "She deserved that. What kind of girlfriend expects her boyfriend to skip out on his family just because she suddenly needed to be entertained?"

"She wasn't really my girlfriend," Jamie said, somewhat defensively. "Anyway, I think we're done. My soul does feel a bit buggered."

Luke chuckled.

"And you've neatly deflected the conversation from Kelsey. Well done." There was a hint of admiration in Jamie's tone. Luke stifled a smug smile.

As they neared the winery, Hayden came to meet them.

"Why aren't you guys working?" he asked without heat.

"Too bloody hot," Jamie said. "I need some water; then I'll get back at it."

Hayden looked toward Luke. "When do you think it'll be finished?"

"Later in the week, depending on the workforce. It shouldn't be a problem. I just hope the rain holds off." Luke followed the weather as if he were a damned meteorologist.

Hayden pressed his lips together. "Yeah, I saw they're calling for a slight chance come Tuesday. Fingers crossed it's nothing much or stays away altogether."

"Agreed," Jamie said. "One of Dylan's crews will be here Monday to work on the tasting room."

"Right. It's about damn time." Hayden shook his head. "We're so behind schedule on that, and we have our first wine club dinner in just a couple of weeks."

"Do we even have enough people to justify the expense?" Luke asked, looking between Hayden and Jamie, who was the money guy.

"We do, actually," Jamie responded. "Cam's been killing himself to get that club up and running, and Brooke's been helping quite a bit. We're probably going to have to hire her away from the distributor." Cam's girlfriend worked for a distribution company and was selling their wine. However, when she and Cam had grown serious, she'd started helping him out with marketing that went beyond the scope of her duties. None of them minded because it helped West Arch. Plus, they liked her. Still, adding to their employee roster seemed a big step.

Luke peered at Jamie over the top of his sunglasses. "Can we afford that?"

"I'm crunching the numbers. We'll see how much wine this guy can make this year." He jabbed his thumb toward Hayden.

"Hey, that depends on this guy's yield." He pointed his finger at Luke.

"Oh, so now it's all on me? I better produce so you can pay for stuff. No pressure." He had a good idea of what their yield would be, but he wouldn't relax until everything was off the vine and appropriately staged in cold storage or in tanks in the winery. "On that note, I'm going back to work. Get your asses back in the vineyard." He pressed his sunglasses to the bridge of his nose as both Hayden and Jamie saluted him.

Shaking his head, Luke made his way further up the hill to check on their army of pickers. He kept an eye out for Kelsey but didn't see her. People trickled out over the course of the evening, and he missed her leaving.

His brother's teasing came back to taunt him and he shook it off. Had they been flirting? Maybe. Not that it mattered, since he didn't have time to date anyone anyway.

That didn't stop him from thinking that he'd be sure to stop in at the library. Everyone needed a good book now and then, right?

Chapter Two
♀ ♂

THOUGH IT HAD been three days since Kelsey had picked grapes at the winery on Saturday, her back and arms were just getting back to feeling normal. She'd been surprised when her muscles had hurt the next day—a lot. Given her schedule, she wasn't great about hitting the gym, but she'd thought she was in pretty good shape. Now she had to reassess that opinion. She'd add that to her insurmountable list of things to do. Right after finding a new place to live that wasn't a crap hole.

She glanced around her tiny one-bedroom apartment with its dingy walls and buckling floorboards and, as usual, quickly fled. Thankfully, she worked so much that she was barely home. But then, working so much made it impossible to find a new place in town, since rental property in Ribbon Ridge was tough to come by. In another year or two, she'd hopefully be able to buy a small town house, right after she paid off her student loans. Okay, maybe a year or two wasn't all that realistic.

She jogged down the creaky stairs and pushed out the door, nearly colliding with one of the hair salon customers beelining for the entrance, which was right next to Kelsey's. Living above the salon meant noise and odd smells. It also meant she'd become friendly with the staff, and they gave her a discount.

Probably the best thing about her apartment was that

it was close to the library and even closer to her other job at The Arch and Vine pub, where she waited tables. In less than five minutes, she stepped into the library and went about her morning routine, which today included continuing the work she'd started upstairs yesterday.

The library was currently entirely housed downstairs, with the upstairs serving as storage and a meeting space that was available to the community during library hours. It had been used only once or twice, which was a good thing since Kelsey and her friends had sort of commandeered it as their headquarters while they researched the history of Ribbon Ridge for the exhibit that would open in January. Nearly half of the upstairs was dedicated to the exhibit space, and the display tables—generously donated by the Archer family—had been delivered on Friday.

Kelsey had spent all of yesterday here setting up the displays beneath the glass in the tables. Mondays were typically her day off, but she nearly always worked here. Hmm, maybe her sore back wasn't just a result of picking grapes. She quickly picked up where she'd left off, organizing a series of photos.

Thankfully, she'd remembered to set an alarm on her phone so she didn't miss opening the library. The groovy synthetic sound interrupted her activity, and she jumped up. Grabbing her phone, she went downstairs to unlock the door. There was already a pair of moms, each with a kid in tow who were literally bouncing as they waited to come inside.

"Good morning!" one of the moms said, smiling. "We're early for story time. They couldn't wait." She gestured to the kids, who were already dashing to the children's reading nook, which Kelsey had set up with a grouping of bean bags as well as two small tables with chairs. The kids plopped onto the bean bags and waited expectantly.

Kelsey laughed. Story time wasn't technically for another thirty minutes, but she understood their excitement. Going to the library had been one of the highlights of her childhood. It was the very reason she'd become a librarian in the first place. "Who am I to keep them waiting?"

"Oh, you don't have to start now," the other mother said, blushing. "We can wait."

"It's no problem," Kelsey said.

"But what if other children come? We don't want them to miss out."

"They won't," Kelsey assured her. "The one thing I can just about guarantee is that we won't run out of books to read." At least not before the kids grew antsy and needed to go home for lunch.

Kelsey went to the children's nook and sat in the rocking chair situated in the corner. The books she'd chosen for today were on the table beside her.

One of the children, a girl with bright blonde hair in pigtails, pointed at the book on the top of the stack. "I love that one!"

Holding it up, Kelsey nodded. "Me too."

The boy stuck out his tongue. "It's about a princess."

"She's a very good princess," the girl said rather haughtily.

"She's still a princess," the boy muttered.

"Never fear," Kelsey said, giving the boy a sly smile. "The next book is about a dragon."

The boy's eyes lit, and both kids' attention grew rapt as Kelsey began to read.

A few more children joined the group, and by the

time the official story time was over, she'd been reading for almost an hour. She needed some water.

After hydrating, she got caught up helping a few people, and before she knew it, her volunteer helper for the afternoon had arrived. Which meant it was one o'clock. No wonder her stomach was growling.

It was also time for Alaina, Crystal, and Brooke to arrive for their meeting. Brooke Ellis strolled in right on time, her blonde hair pulled back into a sleek ponytail. She whipped her sunglasses off and smiled at Kelsey. "Hi! You recovered from Saturday?"

"Barely," Kelsey said, her gaze drifting to the new sparkly diamond on Brooke's left hand. "Are *you*?"

Brooke saw where Kelsey was looking, and her smile widened. "Sort of. It's still a bit surreal. I did manage to give notice at my loft, though." Her eyes rounded. "Oh! You should rent it. I know you're looking for a place."

The loft was a bit out of Kelsey's price range. She could afford it, but she wouldn't be able to save enough to buy her own place. She preferred to put up with her lousy apartment in the short-term in exchange for the long-term gain. "Thanks, but I've decided I'm good at hair salon central."

"Okay, but if you decide to change your mind, do it fast. The loft won't last."

Kelsey and Brooke had been friends for a couple of months, but Kelsey hadn't told her that she lived in the apartment due to financial necessity. Kelsey was by nature a private person, and even more so after what she'd gone through two years ago.

The door opened again, and in walked Crystal Donovan and Alaina Pierce—rather, Alaina Archer. Even though Kelsey considered her a friend, it was hard not to think of the hugely famous actress by anything other than her movie-star name.

Truly best friends forever, Crystal and Alaina often arrived together, which made sense since Crystal stayed with Alaina when she was in town. Crystal wasn't really an official Ribbon Ridge resident since her primary residence was in LA.

Crystal hefted a bag. "Hey, girls! As promised, we brought sandwiches from Barley and Bran."

"Let's head upstairs," Kelsey said, leading the way.

As they reached the top, Kelsey headed toward the meeting room in the far right corner, but her companions walked en masse toward the exhibit space, which spanned the left side of the massive room.

Alaina went to a display table and ran her fingertips along the edge. "Wow, Kelsey, you've gotten a lot done. Didn't the tables just get here on Friday?"

"Yeah, I probably worked too much yesterday."

"You always work too much," Brooke said, shaking her head from another of the tables. "We need to take you away for a girls' weekend."

Kelsey laughed. "Like you'd leave Cameron."

Brooke grinned. "I would. Absence makes the heart grow fonder, after all."

Crystal had also moved to the one of the tables and looked up, her gaze roving among the others. "That's a great idea. Let's go to the beach. I love the Oregon coast in the fall."

"Me too," Alaina said. "And I'm sure we can use the Archers' house."

As much as Kelsey wanted a weekend away, she couldn't leave the library. She had a few volunteers and one newish part-time employee, whose first full day without Kelsey had been Saturday when Kelsey had gone to pick grapes at West Arch. "Sounds fun, but I don't think I can get away for that long. At least not from the library."

"You have help, right?" Crystal asked, tucking a lock of pale blonde hair behind her ear. "You deserve a break, Kel!"

Kelsey couldn't really argue with that. But part of her still had to pinch herself and wonder what she was doing here in this idyllic town, hanging out with a great group of new friends, one of whom just happened to be an A-list celebrity. When Kelsey thought of what she'd come from or where she'd been headed… Well, she tried not to think about that.

She also refused to be pushed into something she didn't want to do. That was the old Kelsey. "I'll think about it. In the meantime, let's eat. I'm starving!"

She went into the meeting room, where a large table dominated the center. Bookshelves lined one wall, a small almost-kitchen with a sink, dishwasher, and fridge took up another wall, and boxes cluttered the corners. Photographs and documents were piled on the table, which Kelsey had been using to sort and organize. She scooted everything to one end to clear a place to eat, then grabbed paper plates from a cupboard.

Brooke pulled various drinks from the fridge—water for her and Alaina, iced tea for Crystal, and a Diet Coke for Kelsey. They'd stocked up on their favorite beverages not long after their meetings about the history exhibit had become somewhat regular.

Crystal set the bag of sandwiches down. "You trust us to eat around that stuff?" She gestured toward the stacks Kelsey had moved over.

"Should I not?" Kelsey asked.

Alaina opened the bag and passed around the

sandwiches, each marked with everyone's initials to differentiate the order. She tossed her BFF a gimlet eye. "We'll be good. This expectant mama needs some protein." Alaina had just announced her pregnancy that weekend at the harvest event. Between that and Cameron and Brooke's engagement, it had been an evening of celebration following the picking—until their collective exhaustion had kicked in and ended the festivities by about ten.

"Besides," Alaina continued, "I'm an expert at keeping mess contained. Comes with having a toddler."

Crystal laughed. "That's because Alexa is the neatest toddler to ever live. I really hope your next child is a whirling dervish."

Alaina rolled her eyes. "Thanks. I'll be sure and have you babysit more often."

Kelsey glanced at Brooke to see how she was taking this kid talk. She'd confided to them that she wasn't able to have children but desperately wanted to. She and Cameron were exploring options. Brooke caught her eye and gave a subtle nod along with a smile. She was good.

Kelsey relaxed. She hated to see anyone in pain.

After a few minutes of eating, Crystal asked, "So what's our plan today besides helping Kelsey with setting up some exhibits? Although it doesn't look like she left us much to do." She flashed Kelsey a wink and a smile.

Kelsey nodded toward the pile on the table and then toward the boxes in the corners. "There's *plenty* to do."

"I have something to report," Alaina said. "I talked to the county historical society, and we have an appointment Friday morning at nine." She took a bite of her sandwich.

Brooke grinned. "Excellent! Did you learn anything about what kinds of maps they have?"

Alaina swallowed and then took a drink of water. "He said they have one of the area, including Ribbon Ridge, circa 1880."

Kelsey was delighted to hear they had a map from that time period. Maybe she could even convince the county to loan it to her for the exhibit. "So it should have Bird's Nest Ranch since it was built in 1879?"

Alaina nodded. "It should, but I guess we'll find out for sure on Friday."

"Then what do we do?" Crystal asked. "It's all well and good to determine where the house stood, but what do we do with that? And how is it going to help us find out what happened to Dorinda Olsen?"

Using a diary provided by the Archer family, their little amateur research team had learned that Dorinda and her husband Hiram had built Bird's Nest Ranch. Hiram had died of a fever, but they hadn't found any documents indicating what had happened to Dorinda.

"I don't know why, but I feel like there's an important story with Dorinda," Crystal said.

Kelsey agreed. The diary entry they'd read about the Olsens had pulled at their heartstrings. Things had seemed rather bleak for them and then Hiram had died.

"I just want to know that she had a happy ending," Brooke said, her brow creasing.

They fell silent for a moment and continued to eat. The sound of someone biting into a potato chip broke the quiet and provoked a giggle from Crystal, who'd caused the noise. "Sorry."

They smiled in return, and the atmosphere warmed again.

Brooke sipped her water. "So, Crystal, you were

asking what we do with this information—assuming we find the house. We've talked about hiring an archaeologist to excavate the site. Are we still thinking we want to do that?" She looked around the table.

"I'd like to, and I'll fund it," Alaina offered.

She offered to pay for everything, which was kind and generous, and she could definitely afford it. Kelsey wished she could make that kind of overture. If she had wealth, she'd share it.

Kelsey smiled at her. "Thank you, Alaina, that's very nice of you. However, we'll need to talk to the guys at West Arch." She looked toward Brooke, since she was engaged to one of the owners.

"I mentioned it to Cam, and he's fine with it, provided it doesn't interfere with their vines."

Kelsey looked toward Brooke. "Luke said the same thing."

Brooke arched a brow at her. "Did he tell you that on Saturday? I heard you were hanging out in the pumpkin patch."

Kelsey felt a need to clarify that situation, though she couldn't say why. "We weren't hanging out, just chatting for a few minutes. We did talk about Bird's Nest Ranch—briefly. He wasn't enthused if it meant disrupting his vineyard. Which I can understand."

"Me too," Alaina said.

Crystal looked around at the others. "Well, fingers crossed the house isn't in the vineyard. There's more to the property than where the grapes are planted, right?"

"Yes." Brooke propped her elbow on the table and leaned her chin on her hand. "The photograph we have of the ranch looks like it's on the top of the slope, but it's hard to tell. Most of that is vineyard, unfortunately. But there are some unplanted areas. For now—they plan to expand later this fall."

Crystal slapped her palm on the table. "Then we'd better get moving." Her expression fell. "What if the house was located where the winery is?"

No one said anything as they exchanged looks. Finally, their collective exhales filled the room.

"In that case, we're done," Kelsey said softly.

Everyone nodded in agreement.

"I'm going back to hoping the house is in a really convenient location. Like that pumpkin patch."

Kelsey thought about Luke's excitement about having it and hoped the site wasn't located there. "I think Luke might be as passionate about his pumpkins as he is about his grapes."

"Really?" Brooke asked, studying her with interest. "What else did you learn about Luke?"

Kelsey felt the blush warm her cheeks but willed it to die down before anyone took notice. Too late—she could see their gazes perking with interest. "Nothing. Like I said, we just chatted for a few minutes."

"Oh." Brooke sounded a little disappointed. "Luke's a great guy. If you were interested."

"I'm not." Kelsey rushed to add, "But I know he's a great guy. I'm just too busy for that kind of thing. Remember, I'm a workaholic." She smiled and took a bite of sandwich while inwardly hoping they'd change the subject.

Thankfully, Alaina bought the clue and went back to talking about their appointment with the historian on Friday. Meanwhile, Kelsey's mind drifted to Luke. He *was* a great guy. And she probably would be interested in him *if* she were interested in any guy. Which she wasn't and didn't expect to be ever again. Noah had pretty much ruined that for her, the bastard.

So Right

He'd caused her so much pain, and it had taken two years to get to the point where she could really even have friends again because her trust had been so battered. Before the library had opened a couple of months ago, she'd worked a second job at a twenty-four-hour store in a neighboring town, as much for something to keep herself busy as for the money. Keeping busy was how she'd coped. Now, keeping busy was simply the way she lived. And for that, she was grateful, because an idle mind focused on dark things. Things better left in the past. Things Kelsey never wanted to think about again.

Chapter Three
❦

IT WAS DARK by the time Luke walked into The Arch and Vine in downtown Ribbon Ridge on Tuesday night. It was Tuesday, right? He'd been working practically nonstop for more than a week. All the grapes would be picked by Sunday, and then he was going to take a day—or hell, maybe even *two*—off.

But right now, he'd settle for a burger and a beer, and not necessarily in that order. Okay, definitely not in that order. He strode straight for the bar, which sat in the middle of the pub. Behind it stood everyone's surrogate fun uncle, George Wilson. A retired marine, he was as much a fixture of Ribbon Ridge as the grapes on the surrounding hillsides or the Archer family, who owned this pub and much of the town.

"Evening, Luke," George said, coming forward and slapping his hand on the bar. "What'll it be tonight, Arrowhead or Crossbow?"

Those were generally his go-to beers, but he was really digging their seasonal. "Actually, I'll take a pint of the Hunter if you have it."

"Of course we have it. It's fall, silly boy." George grinned as he grabbed a glass from the shelf above his gray, buzz-cut head and went to the tap. "Dinner while you're at it?"

"Absolutely. You taking orders tonight, or is one of the servers around?" He peered around the restaurant in search of Kelsey but only saw Andy, who'd started here over the summer.

George adjusted his wire-rimmed glasses on his nose. "I think it's just me and Andy right now. Kelsey's here, but she just left for a break."

Damn. Luke would've liked to invite her to join him. "I'll just take a cheeseburger with buffalo tots."

George set Luke's pint in front of him. "You got it."

Just then, Kelsey came from the back, carrying a salad in one hand and her phone in the other. She was looking at the screen as she walked.

Luke scooped up his beer and intercepted her. "Careful, that's an accident waiting to happen."

She jolted, and he reached out to steady the salad. Her gaze jumped to his, and she frowned slightly. "Were you trying to scare me?"

Shit, no. Now he felt like an ass. This was what happened when introverts tried to get cute. "No, sorry. Totally mangled attempt at flirting. I, uh, was wondering if you wanted to eat with me. George said you were on break."

Her eyes widened slightly after he'd said flirting. He wasn't sure what to make of that. Good reaction or bad one? She glanced around, perhaps looking for an escape route, but since her salad clearly wasn't a to-go order, she was kind of screwed.

He didn't want to be the cause of that. "Actually, maybe I'll just get my burger to go."

She shook her head, and her features relaxed into a smile. "No, don't do that. I'm eating. You're eating. We may as well eat together."

He nearly exhaled with relief but instead simply smiled in return. "Excellent. Lead the way."

She went to a table in the corner. It was dim and out of the way. "Is this okay? I tend to sit in the shadows on break. That way people might forget I'm here, and then I can enjoy my dinner."

Made sense. "This is great. I'm just happy to sit. And drink beer. And eat." *And be with you.*

Really? He asked himself if he'd come here with the hope of seeing her. He hadn't consciously thought so, but in retrospect, it seemed obvious. He liked her, and he wanted to get to know her better.

She slid into the side of the booth that backed up to the wall. "Did George take your order?"

Luke took the bench opposite her and sipped his beer before setting his glass on the table. "Yes."

She winced—it was quick, but Luke caught it.

"Should I be worried? He's taken my order for years."

"Duh, of course he has. You'll be fine. He doesn't do so well with special requests. Don't ask for light dressing or extra pickles."

Luke nodded. "I'll remember that. Though it won't matter to me. I'll eat just about anything." His stomach growled as if to punctuate his statement. He nodded toward her salad. It was huge and packed with all sorts of stuff he'd never seen together in a salad here. "Is that a new addition to the menu?"

She picked up her fork. "No. It's the Kelsey Special. That's one perk of being an employee—you can make whatever the heck you want."

He considered making some flirtatious remark about wanting a Kelsey Special for himself, but thankfully realized he would butcher it the same way he'd done earlier. He settled for taking a drink of beer.

After crunching through a bite of salad, she waved her fork toward him. "How's the harvest going? You about done?"

"Not quite." He picked up his glass to take a drink. "I don't suppose you want to come pick grapes again this weekend?"

"Actually, I would, but I have to work."

He set his glass back down. "Here or the library?"

"Both." She took another bite of salad.

He leaned against the wooden back of the booth. "Do you ever get a day off? I guess that's a stupid question, because you did last Saturday."

She nodded as she swiped her napkin over her mouth. "That was a special case actually. I hired a part-time employee at the library last month because, yes, it would be nice to take a day off now and again." She chuckled. "I do take days off. Okay, *day* off. Mondays. The library's closed Mondays and Wednesdays, so I told myself that I should take at least one of them off both of my jobs."

"Damn, you work as much as I do." He grinned, always glad to find a kindred spirit. "But then I know we're both introverts, and working too much is just part and parcel of that, isn't it?"

"It can be, yes. I didn't always used to work this much, though." She dropped her gaze to her salad and gathered up what looked like some specific items for a savory mouthful.

"What changed?" He wrapped his hand around the base of his glass as he waited for her to finish chewing.

She shrugged. "I don't know. The library, I guess?"

The way she looked off to the side and then refocused on her salad gave him the impression she *did* know and maybe just didn't want to say. The introvert in him sure as hell wasn't going to press her on it.

He recalled a conversation they'd had at some point in their acquaintance in which she'd said she'd always wanted to be a librarian. "Will you be able to work at the library full-time some day?"

"I'm pretty close to that. What would be better is if I could have a second full-time person, but I don't know that Ribbon Ridge has the infrastructure to afford that. My salary is heavily subsidized by a grant from Archer Enterprises as it is."

Ah yes, the Archers—an economy unto themselves. Not that Luke would complain. They were incredibly generous with their time and money, and no one loved Ribbon Ridge more than them. "Well, you never know what the future holds. And it sounds like you're doing an incredible job with it. I still need to stop in." He gave her a sheepish look.

"Whenever. It's not going anywhere." She moved her salad around with her fork. "Anyway, sounds like you're really busy."

George brought Luke's burger and a soft drink that he set in front of Kelsey. He winked at her. "You forgot your Diet Coke again." He looked toward Luke. "She always does that."

"Not *always*," she protested with a smile. "But thank you. I really appreciate it."

He chuckled. "Someone's got to look after you," he said before returning to the bar.

"Things will calm down a little after the harvest is done," Luke said. "Then it'll be Hayden's show."

She sipped her Diet Coke. "What do you do after the harvest—in the winter? I imagine you're far less busy."

"Yes, but there's still plenty to do. I'll plant new vines in November." He started in on his burger.

"Really? I didn't realize you could plant that time of year."

He waited to answer until he swallowed. "Yep, but

So Right

then things do slow down for a while. I take my vacation in the winter."

"That's great if you like to ski, unless you go somewhere tropical." Her eyes took on a dreamy, far-off look. "That sounds lovely."

He set his burger down and wiped his mouth. "I do like to ski, actually. I typically go on some sort of outdoor adventure. I've done a combination climbing and ski trip. That was intense. Last winter, I went to Costa Rica."

"Well, that qualifies as tropical to me—and exotic. But then, Florida qualifies as exotic to me too." She laughed. "I've never been off the West Coast."

He swallowed his tater tot and stared at her. "Seriously?"

She nodded. "Seriously."

He shook his head as he picked up his beer. "That's not right. I'd urge you to go somewhere—hell, I'd offer to take you—but I somehow think you wouldn't take the time off."

She smiled. "I would, but I can't. Not yet anyway. Maybe when my part-time employee has a little more experience. And I'd have to make sure she could even work that much. She's a grad student."

Did she just agree to go on a vacation with him? Or was she only referring to taking time off? Did he really want to take her on a vacation? That seemed, uh, to be rushing things just a bit. "You have two jobs, and you make it work."

She smiled. "True." She asked him about Costa Rica as they finished eating, and by the time his burger was gone, the conversation had turned to hiking in general.

"Sounds like you spend a great deal of time outdoors," she said.

He nodded as he pushed his plate to the side. "As much as I can. It's one of the reasons I love my job so much. If I couldn't do this, I'd be a park ranger, probably."

"You must love living here—in the Pacific Northwest."

"I do. I went to school in northern California and worked there for several years. I admit I'm glad to be home."

"Sadly, I have to get back to work," she said. "Before I go, I wanted to let you know that we're going to the county historical society on Friday to look at maps of the vineyard. Before it was a vineyard."

He polished off his beer. "Oh?"

"Yes, we hope the map will show us where the Bird's Nest Ranch house was located."

She looked so eager. He tamped down his uncertainty. "Hopefully not in my vineyard."

"Agreed." She cast him an apprehensive glance. "We plan to consult with an archaeologist after we determine the location. Of course we'll include you."

"Thanks. Just let me know what you need, and we'll do our best to accommodate you."

"I really appreciate that. And I promise we won't disrupt your vines. I get it." She gave him a warm smile, and he knew she did, in fact, get it. She sucked down the rest of her Diet Coke and started to rise. "Time to get back to work."

Disappointment swirled in his gut. There was more he wanted to talk about with her. More he wanted to know about her. He stood and joined her next to the booth. Since taking a vacation together had come up— even if it was a joke—he thought they should maybe start with something far simpler. "Hey, since you don't work on Mondays, do you want to go hiking with me? I'll be done with the harvest, so I'm going to take the day off. I'd planned to go up to Gales Creek."

She hesitated, and he was sure she was going to say no. "I usually work at the library on Mondays—yes, even on my day off. And I have a lot to do for this exhibit. Thanks for the offer, though."

No it was, then. He didn't want to accept that answer. "Is it critical you work on Monday? I mean, if *I* can take a day off, you can too, right?"

She paused again, as if her mind was churning. He recognized that look because he was a master—come up with something quick so you could avoid whatever event was being proposed. "Look, I don't want you to get the wrong idea. I'm just not interested."

Ouch.

ॐ

KELSEY WATCHED THE disappointment crest over his features and felt a pang of regret. She liked him, but she just couldn't date anyone. Crap, she really ought to clarify that.

"Interested in dating, I mean." She shook her head, feeling like an idiot. "You're a great guy. Or so you seem. So people tell me. I'm just… I'm just not dating."

His expression relaxed. "I see."

"I really hope we can be friends."

"Definitely." His brow furrowed briefly before he smiled at her. "I thought we were already."

Well, duh, of course they were. She was completely butchering this. "Right!"

"Good luck on Friday, and let us know how it goes. See you later."

She watched him leave and noted that he'd said to let "us" know, not him. What did she expect? He'd asked her out, and she'd turned him down. He'd get over it, but that didn't make the moment any less awkward. She hoped it was just that—a moment—and they could be friends. Continue being friends.

Ugh, she was a dork. This was what happened when you tried to reenter the social world after self-imposed isolation.

She bussed their table and immersed herself in work. The pub wasn't very busy, but there were always projects to do, such as cleaning under tables and chairs. So disgusting, but necessary.

"Kelsey!" George's voice interrupted her attempt to pry gum from the bottom of a booth.

She popped her head up and gasped. Standing ten feet from her was the face she loved most in the world—her Grandma Ruby.

"Gram!" She jumped to her feet and rushed forward but stopped before reaching her. "I'd hug you, but my hands are gross."

Gram's brown eyes twinkled as she smiled. "I don't care about that. Give me a hug."

Kelsey wrapped her arms around her grandmother, who was a good two inches shorter than Kelsey's five feet six. She inhaled the familiar scent of Gram's perfume—Giorgio Beverly Hills—and felt something she hadn't in years: a sense of home.

When she finally pulled back, she asked, "What on earth are you doing here?"

Gram lived in Chehalis, Washington, more than two hours away. She waved her hand. "Couldn't stand another day with your mother and Todd." She rolled her eyes. "Save me."

Kelsey tried to process what she was saying. "How? You came to stay?"

"For a little while. Until I can figure out what I want to do."

An image of welcoming Gram to her tiny, horrible apartment made Kelsey cringe. But of course Gram could stay. Kelsey understood the need to escape her parents. She'd give Gram her bed and sleep on the couch as long as necessary. "I'm surprised you lasted six months, actually." Gram had sold her house and surrounding property last spring and had moved in with Kelsey's folks for the short-term.

"They liked having me there. Because I was a free babysitter for Malcolm." Gram said, scoffing. "I love that boy, but I have my own life! Or at least I used to. I'm not sure Chehalis is big enough for me and your mother."

Boy, did Kelsey get that. It hadn't been for her and Wendy, which was why Kelsey had graduated high school early and taken off for college at seventeen. "I'm sorry."

"Eh, I should've known better. That's what I get for getting soft in my old age."

"Old age, schmold age," George said, stepping closer to them. "I've got years on you, beautiful, and I'm not old."

Kelsey smiled at this and also at his calling Gram "beautiful." "Actually, George, I think you're older than my grandmother by a year or so. Gram, this is George Wilson. George, this is my grandmother Ruby Atwood."

George took her hand and gave it a squeeze. "The

pleasure is mine. I'm certain your granddaughter is fibbing." He tossed Kelsey a humor-filled glance. "She likes to try to pull one over on me."

"Ha!" Kelsey chuckled. "You're the one who does that, not me. Don't listen to him, Gram, he's incorrigible."

Gram's lips curved up as she surveyed him. "I like incorrigible," she murmured.

George's chest seemed to swell, and he looked as if he grew an inch taller. "Will you be visiting Ribbon Ridge for a bit, Miss Atwood?"

The sound of Gram's girlish laughter made Kelsey's eyebrows arch. "Oh, you call me Ruby. Everyone does. Yes, I'll be visiting for a bit. Are you my precious granddaughter's boss?"

"No, they don't want me running this joint!" He leaned close and affected a stage whisper. "The truth is, I don't want to run this joint." He winked at her, something he did often, but it seemed slightly different this time.

Kelsey wasn't sure what to make of this flirt fest. It was cute as hell, but she was still trying to process having Gram here. Kelsey was equal parts thrilled and overwhelmed. Which was silly. Gram wouldn't be a burden. Growing up, she'd been Kelsey's biggest cheerleader.

"I bet you could manage this place with both hands tied behind your back," Gram said. Was she fluttering her eyelashes?

Kelsey cleared her throat. "So, uh, Gram, I'm working until ten thirty tonight. If you want, I can give you the key to my place." She hated sending her over there by herself. But maybe it was best if Kelsey didn't see Gram's expression when she went inside.

"Oh, forget that," George said gruffly. "Take the rest of the night off."

"I thought you weren't in charge," Gram said.

"Eh, the assistant manager is here tonight, and he'll agree with me. We're not that busy. I'm pretty sure whatever gunk she was cleaning from the bottom of that booth will be there tomorrow."

Kelsey didn't typically like to go home early. She had a strict budget, and working fewer hours meant it took longer to pay off her student loans. However, it was only a little money and she was looking forward to spending time with Gram. "Are you sure?" she asked him.

"I insist. Go on, then." He nodded toward the back, where they had lockers. "I'll keep Ruby company while you get your things."

"And wash your hands," Gram added.

Kelsey laughed softly. "Definitely washing my hands. Thanks, George." She started toward the back, casting a backward glance at the two of them as George guided Gram to the bar. Kelsey decided to take her time.

About ten minutes later, after clearing her early departure with the assistant manager, Kelsey walked to the bar, where Gram was just finishing a sample of something. "George, are you plying my grandmother with alcohol?"

His dark gray brows shot up his forehead. "She can't come in to the Archers' flagship pub and not try some beer."

Kelsey had to agree with that.

Gram set her empty glass on the bar. "There you are, dear. I was beginning to think you'd forgotten me." Her teasing smile said she didn't think that at all.

"I'm ready if you are." The way things were going

between Gram and George, Kelsey could see Gram wanting to stay a bit longer.

"Oh, I'm ready. It was a long drive from Chehalis. There was an accident on the I-5 bridge."

That had to have added at least an hour to her trip. "Sorry to hear that. I'll make you some cocoa when we get to the apartment." Kelsey had fond memories of Gram making her hot cocoa with fluffy marshmallows. Now she could return the favor. Except she was pretty sure she only had envelopes of cocoa with those tiny marshmallows that were anything but fluffy. Not quite the same thing.

Gram chuckled. "Sounds good." She hopped off her barstool, proving that age was just a number, and flashed George a smile. "I will see you around, Mr. Wilson."

"I'll look forward to it, Ruby. And since we're first-naming here, you'd better call me George. Or Lummox. That works too."

Everyone laughed, and Kelsey led Gram from the pub. Once outside, she turned her head to look at her grandmother in wonder. "I've never seen you flirt before."

"That's because Grandpa was always around." He'd died only about two and a half years ago. They'd had a warm, loving marriage, but this was a different side of Gram. "Although I think we flirted. Didn't we?"

"Yes, but that was to be expected—you were Gram and Grandpa! My apartment is there." She pointed to the building across the street and gestured for them to cross, but stopped short at the curb. "Wait, where are you parked?"

"In the lot behind the pub," she said. "I'll need to move it to your parking lot or wherever it is you keep your car. Do you really live there?" Her gaze went back to the old building that Kelsey called home.

"Yes, and, uh, the parking is a problem. My apartment doesn't have a lot or a garage." She actually paid the auto shop four blocks away to keep her car in their lot.

The wrinkles in Gram's brow formed deeper crevices as she frowned. "I see. I suppose I should've let you know I was coming. I just got a bee in my bonnet, I guess. Well, where can I park for tonight? Tomorrow, I should probably head back to Chehalis."

Kelsey hated the resigned tone in Gram's voice, and she wasn't going to let her suffer with Mom and Todd. "Nonsense. You can stay as long as you like." She might change her mind once she saw Kelsey's apartment, but it was still probably better than Mom and Todd's house. "I'm just going to dash back inside and tell George about your car. You can leave it there overnight. We'll figure something else out tomorrow."

"I'll need my bags too," Gram called after her. "I left them in my car."

A few minutes later, with Gram's luggage in tow, they crossed the street and Kelsey unlocked the door to the stairs leading up to her apartment. She insisted that Gram go on up with just her small bag, and Kelsey would manage the two larger ones in separate trips. Gram went first, and Kelsey followed, dragging the rolling suitcase up the rickety stairs.

"One of your lights is out here," Gram said as she neared the top. There were three lights in the stairwell, and the middle one had needed replacement for going on two months. Kelsey's landlord was incredibly nonresponsive. But he sure cashed her rent checks on time.

"I know. The landlord said he'd fix it soon."

Gram made a soft grunt as she walked to the door to the apartment and waited for Kelsey.

Kelsey pulled out her key and gave Gram a bracing look. "It's not much, okay?"

Gram nodded, her features determined. "I'm sure it's very nice."

Ha, not even close.

Kelsey opened the door and pushed it wide so Gram could precede her. She trailed her inside, pulling Gram's case. She didn't wait to see or hear Gram's reaction. "I'll just run down and get the other one."

After parking the second suitcase in her small living room, Kelsey shut the door and bolted the lock. "Home sweet home."

Gram's eyes were wide as she turned to look at Kelsey. "There's nothing 'sweet' about this, honey. What on earth are you doing living here?"

"Um, it's all I can afford?"

"I had no idea! Why didn't you tell me? I'm not poor, you know."

Yes, she knew. Just as she knew Gram wasn't wealthy either. She lived a comfortable but modest life, and she deserved to enjoy her life savings, not subsidize her granddaughter.

"There's nothing to tell, Gram," Kelsey said, trying not to sound defensive. It wasn't *that* bad after all. And it was a sure sight better than her previous situation, even if she had been living in a nice house in one of the newer neighborhoods outside McMinnville, which was about fifteen minutes from Ribbon Ridge. "I'm comfortable and safe, and for now, it works."

Gram didn't appear convinced as her gaze roamed the small space. "At least your furniture is nice, even if you don't have much of it. What happened to everything you and Noah had? I bought you a nice kitchen table when you moved here."

Kelsey took a deep breath. She hated talking about Noah but knew he was bound to come up. "He ran up a bunch of debt in my name. I had to sell a lot of things to pay everything off." And she'd finally settled the last credit card bill a few months ago, which just left her student loans.

Gram gasped softly and moved toward Kelsey. "Kelsey honey, why haven't you said anything? What you went through with him was bad enough. I know you're extremely independent—always have been—but sometimes you just have to let family help you."

That was easier said than done, especially when your own mother said you had to live with your mistakes. And independent? Noah had made sure she wasn't. Which had made it especially important for Kelsey to pick herself up.

Kelsey moved past Gram and set her purse on the small kitchen table she'd picked up at Goodwill. "You were busy with Grandpa. He was really sick when all that was happening."

That had been the worst year. All the problems with Noah and then losing Grandpa... Kelsey really didn't want to revisit any of it. She spun around and gave Gram a bright smile. "Anyway, it's all in the past, and I'm doing really well. I love living here, and the new library is going great."

Gram came toward her and took her hand. "I'm glad, dear. It makes me so happy that you're finally pursuing what you've always wanted."

"Thank you." She gave Gram's hand a squeeze before letting it go. "So, I only have one bedroom. I want you to take the bed, and I'll take the couch."

Gram turned her head to look at the living room, which was only large enough for the couch, a small coffee table, and a floor lamp. "I feel terrible for intruding on you like this."

"Please don't. It's actually nice to have company." Kelsey had never invited anyone up here. She'd been too embarrassed for people to see how she lived, but having Gram here gave her courage—and peace. "Come on, I'll show you the bedroom and bathroom."

"Okay, but Kelsey?" Gram's features hardened. "If I ever get my hands on that Noah Putnam, he's going to wish he'd never been born."

Only if Kelsey didn't get a shot at him first.

Chapter Four

❧

"GET THE FUCK out of the bathroom!" Luke yelled as he pounded on the door for the third time.

"Language!" Jamie responded loudly, citing their mother's oft-repeated admonishment. "You could ask nicely."

"Get the fuck out of the bathroom, *please.*" Luke slammed his fist against the wood again. "You said you'd be ten minutes. That was twenty minutes ago. Meanwhile, I'm going to crawl out of my skin if I don't get this dirt off me." He'd come from the vineyard without showering at the winery, which he typically did. He'd wanted to get home because their mom was bringing them dinner tonight, something she insisted on doing from time to time, much to their appreciation.

At last, the door opened. And Jamie came striding out with a smug little-brother look on his face. "I made sure to leave you plenty of hot water."

"Gee, thanks." Luke scowled at him as he went into the bathroom to take his long-awaited and much-needed shower.

Fifteen minutes later, after he was clean and dressed, he stalked into the kitchen and went straight for the fridge and a beer. He popped the top off and turned to glare at Jamie, who was bent over the *New York Times* crossword puzzle on the kitchen table. "You lied. I ran out of hot water before I even finished rinsing the shampoo from my hair."

"Oops." Jamie filled in some boxes. "I think we need to have the landlord look at the hot water heater."

The landlord lived across the street and was eighty-five years old. "You mean we should have Dylan come look at it? Fred isn't going to fix the damn hot water heater. Anyway, I don't think that's the issue." *It's you using all the hot water.*

Jamie glanced up. "What? Oh. Sorry." He went back to scratching his pencil over the newspaper. He was almost done.

"Did you just start that when I got in the shower?"

"Not quite." He shrugged. "I dunno. I wasn't paying attention."

Typical. Those sorts of details didn't always hit his radar. He was too busy solving crossword puzzles or complex math problems in record time.

The doorbell rang, prompting Luke to lurch away from the counter where he'd been leaning. "Don't get up," he said to Jamie as he walked by.

He opened the door to their mom standing on the mat, her arms laden with her casserole tote and a grocery bag. "Sorry I'm late, I had to stop and get bread, but Barley and Bran was out of sourdough. I had to get the cheaper, mass-produced kind at the store."

She winced, and Luke knew just how much that bothered her. She prided herself on taking care of her boys, and that included giving them the best dinner she could. That sourdough bread mattered more to her than it did to them didn't matter. She *thought* it should matter to them, and so she went the extra mile.

"It's fine, Mom, thanks. Let me take that." He still had a beer in one hand, so he took the grocery bag, which—as he'd expected—held more than just the bread. There was a sealed plastic bowl in the bottom, which certainly held salad. She'd say they needed a balanced meal. If she only knew how they typically ate… Of course she knew. It was why she brought them dinner periodically.

He stepped aside so she could move inside past him, then he closed the door with his foot and sealed it shut with his shoulder.

When they arrived in the kitchen, Jamie was setting the table.

Mom beamed at him, her green gaze shining with pride. "You're such a good boy, Jamie."

Luke rolled his eyes. As the youngest, Jamie was pretty much the golden child. The crossword puzzle was now on the counter, and it was finished. Brilliant golden child at that.

Mom opened her tote to reveal her lasagna, and Luke's stomach growled. She set it in the middle of the table and went to prep the salad next. "I brought dressing. I thought I saw you were low when I was here last week."

Luke and Jamie sat and allowed Mom to wait on them. They stopped protesting and trying to help a long time ago.

She put the salad between them with a pair of tongs. "Here's balsamic for Luke." She set the bottle near his bowl and put a second bottle beside Jamie's. "And bleu cheese for Jamie."

Jamie smiled up at her. "Thanks, Mom."

"I actually bought salad dressing the other day," Luke said. "We do know how to take care of ourselves."

She waved her hand. "Oh, I know you do. I just like to do my part." She smiled and sat down next to Jamie, opposite Luke.

They'd also stopped inviting her to join them since she always declined, having eaten with their dad earlier. Sometimes Dad came with her, but not tonight. He probably had something at the middle school where he was the principal.

"We appreciate it," Luke said, helping himself to a large piece of lasagna. "Thanks, Mom."

They ate for a couple of minutes while Mom caught them up on what she and Dad had been doing this week. Nothing exciting beyond their new cat attacking one of Mom's houseplants.

"You both look like you just showered," she said, glancing back and forth between them. "Did you just get home from work?"

Jamie answered between bites. "Yep."

Mom frowned. "It's eight o'clock. You boys work too much."

Uh-oh, here it came. Luke braced himself as he slid a look toward his brother. Jamie cast his gaze to the ceiling very briefly before sending a brilliant smile toward Mom. "We're young and single. What else should we be doing? Perhaps you'd like it better if we went clubbing or maybe dabbled in drugs?"

Mom's gaze turned icy for a moment, then she waved her hand again. "You're kidding. Stop that. You said it yourself: you're both single. I can hardly believe that your brother is getting married before either one of you."

No one could believe it. Cameron had gone through a bitter breakup after college, and it had taken him the better part of eight years to finally move on. He'd done a lot of clubbing, actually, but no drugs.

Luke picked up his beer and raised it in a toast. "Yay for Cam."

Mom folded her arms across her chest and pursed her lips at both of them. "You're both nice boys. Why aren't you even dating? There are plenty of lovely young women in Ribbon Ridge."

Jamie gave Luke a wide-eyed glance that said he clearly didn't agree with that assessment. Luke fought not to laugh. Ribbon Ridge was a small town. Yes, there were lovely young women here, but "plenty" was perhaps a stretch. An image of Kelsey popped into Luke's head. She was lovely. And young. And very much a woman.

Jamie served himself another helping of lasagna. "Maybe one of us will beat Cam to the altar. They haven't set a wedding date yet."

"Good point," Luke said before crunching a bite of salad. "One of us could have a whirlwind romance and elope."

Jamie nodded. "Like Sean and Tori."

Sean Hennessy and Tori Archer had done just that and kept their marriage secret for months. Luke grinned at their mother, knowing they were torturing her but not able to stop himself. "Hell, maybe one of us is already married."

Now it was Mom's turn to roll her eyes. "You're both terrible." She speared Luke with a sharp look. "Whatever happened with Paige? She was nice."

Luke forked up a bite of lasagna. "She was. She still is, I'm sure."

Mom cocked her head to the side. "Then why did you break up exactly?"

"Because I moved here, and long-distance relationships suck?" Luke didn't want to talk about Paige or why they hadn't worked out. Mom would just pester him even more. "You have to let that go, Mom.

Paige and I simply didn't work out. I'm fine with that. You should be too."

She exhaled. "I suppose." She turned to Jamie. "And you, why aren't you and Madison seeing each other anymore?"

Jamie shrugged. "We simply didn't work out." He winked at Luke as he picked up his beer, and Luke rushed to sweep his bottle from the table so they could toast each other.

"I think you're ganging up on me," Mom said, clearly growing frustrated.

Jamie set his beer down and reached over to touch her elbow. "We're sorry. We're just giving you a hard time, which is kind of what you're doing. We're both busy with work right now. We're happy. We're healthy. It's all good."

"I know. Is it so bad that I just want to see all my boys settled?" She unfolded her arms and patted Jamie's shoulder.

Jamie finally served himself some salad, albeit a rather small helping. "You mean married. We're quite settled, right, Luke?"

Luke wasn't sure he agreed with that, not with their current living arrangement. He loved his brother, but he liked his own space. That he'd endured having him for a roommate for two years kind of blew his mind. However, time and money had factored into the decision to stay together. For now. Luke was just about done.

Feeling suddenly claustrophobic, he stood up and took his plates to the sink. He rinsed them and put them in the dishwasher, leaving it open as an unsubtle hint that Jamie should do the same. He wasn't great at cleaning up after himself.

Mom stood. "I'll go. Enjoy your lasagna. I'll pick up the pan next week." She grabbed the empty casserole tote and leaned down to kiss Jamie's cheek.

Luke moved away from the dishwasher. "I'll walk you out."

She smiled at him. "Thanks."

He held the door for her and closed it behind him once they were outside. The fall evening was cool, but not uncomfortably so. The scent of crisp, dry leaves and a fire from some farmer's property filled the air.

"I'm sorry if I annoyed you," she said as she used her remote to unlock her mini-SUV.

He moved to open the door for her. "You didn't."

"Good. I'm just so surprised at Cam being the first to be engaged and that you and Jamie are still living together. Honestly, your father and I gave you six months before you decided you'd had enough. Maybe you're not as much of a loner as we thought." She eyed him intently as a breeze stirred her blonde hair. She didn't have much gray but was still careful to color it.

He laughed. His folks had always had him pegged. "Oh, I am, and I'm surprised I've lasted this long with Jamie too." He winced. "I don't know how much more I can take, though."

"Oh no, is it bad? It seems like you're getting along so well."

"We are. It's just a small house, and we have different…living styles."

She reached inside the car and set the casserole tote on the passenger seat. "You were always much tidier. What are you going to do?"

"I'm not sure what I *can* do. Good rental property in Ribbon Ridge is tough to come by."

"True. Maybe it's time you bought something. You

can afford it, can't you?"

He could. He'd dumped a lot of money into the winery two years ago, but he had enough to buy something small. If he wanted to. "I'm not sure I'm ready for those kinds of roots."

She touched his arm. "What are you afraid of, Luke? You've always been so careful and so…uninterested in forming deep relationships. You never really had a best friend growing up."

He couldn't dispute anything she said, just as he couldn't answer her question. "I don't think I'm afraid. I'm just…here." Waiting. Yes, waiting. Maybe that was it. He'd settle down, as she put it, when it was right. So far, it hadn't been right.

She leaned forward and kissed his cheek. "I love you. See you soon."

"Love you too. Say hi to Dad."

She climbed into the car with a nod. "Will do."

He watched her fire up the engine and pull out of the driveway. Instead of going back inside, he inhaled the night air and started walking. When he reached Main Street, he paused, realizing he'd given zero thought to his destination. Or if he even had one.

He turned left and found himself approaching The Arch and Vine. Without hesitating, he walked inside and strode to the bar. George must've had the night off because it was another of their bartenders, Mick. He made a killer Moscow mule, so Luke ordered one.

"You got it," he said, grabbing a copper mug from the shelf above his head. "What brings you in here tonight?"

"Just out for a stroll and thought I'd stop in."

Mick mixed the drink with expert hands. "Excellent. So my wife joined your wine club the other day. She's really excited about the dinner coming up."

Right, their first wine club dinner was in a few weeks. "Cool. I'm glad you guys joined."

"Wouldn't miss it. You know how much I love pinot."

Mick didn't look like a wine connoisseur with his tattoos and piercings, but he had a fantastic palate and worked part-time as a sommelier for the wine-and-cheese shop next door.

Just then, Kelsey entered Luke's line of sight. Or had he been looking for her? She took an order at a booth and turned toward the bar. He knew the exact moment she saw him. Her eyes widened slightly, and there seemed to be a hitch in her step.

He felt an answering hitch in his chest. Her beauty threatened to steal his breath. Hell, when had his mild interest in her become something more?

He didn't know, but it had. He'd been utterly disappointed when she'd turned him down last night. And yet here he was, seeking her out—and yes, he could be honest with himself and admit that was exactly what he was doing.

She walked up to the bar. "Mick, I need a Crossbow and a Maid Marion."

Mick set Luke's mule in front of him before grabbing two pint glasses. "You got it."

"Hey, Kelsey," Luke said, picking up his ice-cold copper mug. He sipped the mule, the delicious ginger spice awakening his tongue.

"Hi, Luke, how's it going?"

"Great, thanks." This felt stilted. Awkward. He hated that. He never should've asked her out. Or maybe she should've said yes, a tiny voice argued at the back of his mind. He mentally told that voice to shut the hell up.

"Working again, huh?"

She grinned. "Always. How late did you work tonight?"

"Seven. I cut out early."

She laughed. "Slacker."

He couldn't help but smile. Okay, maybe this wasn't awkward. They could be friends. He was glad.

"Be right back," Mick said. "The Crossbow keg just blew." He unhooked the empty, hefted up over his shoulder, and headed toward the back.

Luke sipped his drink again. "It's a good thing you turned me down the other night. I don't think either one of us has time to date."

Her smile faded, but she nodded. "Very true. And now I have a houseguest. My grandmother is here visiting from Chehalis."

He turned on the barstool to face her. "Is that good or bad?"

"Oh, it's great. It was a surprise, but I'm thrilled to have her here. She's probably the person I feel closest to in the whole world."

He could hear the love in her tone and thought her grandmother must be pretty special. "Lucky her," he said softly.

She blushed slightly. "Yeah, well, we're just close."

"That's nice. How long will she be here?"

"I'm not sure. She doesn't know either. She's currently without a home, actually. She sold her property last spring and was staying with my folks until she couldn't stand it anymore."

Luke thought of his own situation. "I can so relate."

Kelsey's brow shot up. "Oh?"

"I live in a nine-hundred-square-foot house with my brother. One bathroom. You do the math."

She made a face. "Yikes. I get you."

Luke picked up his mug. "Well, it's nice she has you to turn to. Ah, here comes Mick, carrying that keg like it's a nearly weightless blanket."

"I'll go hiking with you."

Luke had brought the mug to his mouth, but his hand stilled. He peered at her over the rim, wondering if he'd heard her correctly or if his hopes had made him hear something that hadn't been said. "What?"

"I said I'd go hiking with you. On Monday."

Warmth spread through his chest as he took a sip of his drink. He set the mug back down on the bar. "Okay. Great. I'll pick you up at ten. Do you have a hydration pack?"

She shook her head. "I don't. Should I get one?"

"No, I have extras. And don't worry about food—I'll take care of everything. Any food allergies?"

She shook her head again.

"Where should I pick you up? I don't know where you live."

She gestured toward the door. "Across the street, basically—over the hair salon. I'll meet you outside."

He smiled at her, so glad he'd decided to come here tonight. "Perfect."

Mick had hooked up the new keg and now brought the two pints over to Kelsey. "Here you go. One Maid Marion cider and one Crossbow fresh off the brand new keg."

"Thanks, Mick." She pushed her hair back behind her ear and swept up the glasses. She looked toward Luke. "See you Monday."

He watched her go and couldn't stop smiling.

Mick came over to where Luke was seated and leaned on the bar across from him. "Did McDade just agree to go out with you?"

"She's joining me for a hike on Monday."

"So that's a yes. Damn, brother, good job. She keeps to herself mostly. It's nice to see her do something social." Mick left to attend to a couple at the other end of the bar.

Luke's gaze found Kelsey bussing a table. They had so much in common. He couldn't help but anticipate spending more time with her. On a date. Because that was exactly what it was.

He held up his mug in her direction and thought to himself: *introverts unite!*

"TURN LEFT HERE," Gram said.

Kelsey put on her signal and made the turn.

"It's just up ahead on the right." Gram looked up from her phone.

Catching sight of the sign that read "County Historical Society," Kelsey pulled into the parking lot. "You're an excellent navigator, Gram."

"Thank you. I've gotten pretty good at using this phone. Malcolm's taught me all the tricks."

Kelsey smiled, marveling at how savvy young kids were with electronics. She saw it all the time at the library as kids sat down at the computers. At that moment, her phone pinged. Since she was still driving, she ignored it, but Gram picked it up and looked at the screen.

"Who's Luke?"

Kelsey parked the car and shut off the engine as her heart picked up a bit of speed. She took the phone from Gram. "Just a friend."

"Who you have a date with?"

The text read: *Can I pick you up at ten thirty instead?*

"It's not a date. We're going hiking." It was sort of a date. Wasn't it? She'd gotten a little thrill when she'd brazenly and rather thoughtlessly blurted that she'd go with him—just like when you agreed to a first date. She hadn't been on very many of those, but she remembered.

She didn't even *want* to date. What was she *thinking?*

Clearly, she hadn't been. Thinking. He'd walked into the pub last night looking all sexy in dark blue jeans and a dark-green T-shirt that had displayed his rugged, athletic frame to drool-worthy effect.

Gram sent her a skeptical glance as she opened her door. "I don't care what you call it, it's a step in the right direction." She smiled before stepping out of the car.

Kelsey wasn't sure it was the right direction, but it was a *step.*

She got out of the car and locked it, then joined Gram in walking to the front door. Once inside, Kelsey smiled. The scent of old paper and curiosity filled her nostrils—the smell of a library. She felt perfectly at home.

"Hi, can I help you?" The question came from a young man behind the front desk.

Kelsey went to the counter. "Yes, we have an appointment with Darryl Gray."

"You're looking at maps today." He smiled at her. "That'll be fun."

"I think so."

The door opened behind Kelsey, and she turned her head to see the other three women enter. They'd offered a ride to Kelsey, but she'd declined since Gram was with her.

"Hello!" Crystal called out. She immediately went to shake Gram's hand. "You must be Kelsey's grandma."

"I am. Please call me Ruby."

"I'm Crystal." She let go of Gram and gestured to introduce Alaina and Brooke.

Gram's eyes rounded. "Oh my goodness, you really are Alaina Pierce. Kelsey told me you were a friend of hers, but I just couldn't quite believe it." She laughed as she sent Kelsey a look of apology.

Alaina laughed. "I'm plain old Alaina Archer around here. It's nice to meet you." She shook Gram's hand, and Gram looked a little starstruck.

"Good morning." A masculine voice broke up their grouping, and they all turned to see the new arrival. He was a beefy fellow, probably in his fifties, with a shock of white-blond hair and wire-rimmed glasses. "I'm Darryl."

Kelsey reached out and shook his hand. "Hi, I'm Kelsey McDade. Thank you so much for meeting with us."

"My pleasure. I have everything ready for you, if you'll just follow me." He led them down a hallway and to the right into a conference room. A large table was covered with several maps.

Darryl moved to one end. "Down here is the oldest map—from 1880. I believe the homestead you're looking for is here." He pointed to a black square on the yellowed paper.

They all gathered around and looked down at the map, which showed the topography of the area as well as what Ribbon Ridge had looked like at that time. There were maybe a dozen black squares around the present-day town.

"Wow, there's hardly anything there," Crystal said.

Darryl nodded. "Early days for Ribbon Ridge. The place you're looking for—the Bird's Nest Ranch—is one of the first homesteads built in the hills." His fingers moved west over the map. "Here's the first one. That belonged to the Archers. This structure is still standing."

"And it's still in use," Alaina said. "My daughter likes to play pretend at what she calls 'the old cabin.'"

"Remarkable." Darryl's tone reflected his keen appreciation. "As you know, the Bird's Nest Ranch is long gone. If you look over the maps, you'll see it just vanishes somewhere between 1901 and 1919. We can't find any maps from between those years, and it's not on the 1919 map." He walked to the other end of the table and smoothed his hand over the place where the homestead would have been.

They moved as a group to the 1919 map. "Well, this gives us something to go on," Brooke said. "At least we can narrow our research to this time frame to try to find out what became of Dorinda."

Crystal looked around at them. "I wonder what happened to the homestead?"

"Don't know," Darryl said. "But I did find a death certificate for Dorinda Olsen. She died in 1902."

There was a collective intake of breath as they all looked at each other. Sadness was reflected in their gazes.

"Did it say how she died?" Brooke asked softly.

Darryl shook his head. "I'm afraid not."

"I don't suppose you could find out if she had any offspring?" Kelsey thought they could maybe track down the family and see if they had any knowledge of what had happened.

"Not that I could find. I admit I did a bit of research since I spoke to you the other day. I love this sort of thing. From what I could dig up, Dorinda's husband, Hiram, died in 1881, and she lived another twenty plus years at Bird's Nest Ranch."

"By herself," Alaina mused aloud, saying what they were probably all thinking.

"I can't imagine her working that land alone," Kelsey said. "But perhaps she had help."

"Or not," Gram interjected. "I ran our little farm for a couple of years after your grandpa passed. Granted, it was just goats and chickens and some trees we sold to a local nursery. My point is, don't discount Dorinda because she was alone, and definitely don't do it because she was a woman." The fire in her gaze warmed Kelsey's heart. Gram was so strong and independent. Hopefully these were traits Kelsey had finally learned to take advantage of.

Alaina looked at the others. "So what do we do now?"

"I'd still like to try to find the house," Crystal said. "Maybe we'll discover something helpful." She moved back to the other end of the table. "This shows us where it was."

They all gravitated back to the first map.

Darryl flicked a look toward Alaina. "Did you say you planned to hire an archaeologist? I can give you some names."

Alaina nodded. "That would be great."

"I'll be back in a few minutes." He walked from the conference room.

They broke off into smaller conversations, and Kelsey took a picture of the location of the Bird's Nest

Ranch homestead with her phone. Then she meandered to the other end of the table to look at the newest map.

Brooke joined her. "Your grandma seems pretty great."

Kelsey looked over at Gram, who was chatting with Crystal. "She is. I'm really glad she came to stay with me."

"Is it a temporary thing?"

Kelsey still wasn't really sure. They hadn't talked about Gram's long-term plans. Probably because Gram didn't have any yet. "I think so."

"Your apartment is only one bedroom, right? If this isn't temporary, you should reconsider my loft—it has two bedrooms."

"I misspoke. It *is* a temporary thing. I just don't know how temporary. Anyway, it's fine. I like having her with me, even if it means sleeping on the couch."

Alaina sidled up to them. "Did I hear you say you're sleeping on the couch? Why?"

"Gram's got the bedroom," Kelsey said. "It's all good. She's just figuring out what she wants to do next."

"Well, if she needs a place to stay for a bit, she could almost certainly stay with the Archers. They have a fantastic apartment out at their place—over the garage. Your grandma would be more than comfortable. I'll ask them about it."

Kelsey shook her head. "Oh, I couldn't possibly intrude."

"You wouldn't be. It's for your grandma. And she wouldn't be intruding either. The Archers *love* helping people." Alaina looked over at Gram. "Hey, Ruby, how'd you like to move into a furnished luxury apartment just outside Ribbon Ridge?"

Gram blinked at her, and Kelsey saw that she was interested. "Does such a thing exist?"

Alaina nodded. "Absolutely. Let me work out the details, but I bet you could be moved in this weekend."

A smile curved Gram's lips. "Oh my goodness, Ribbon Ridge is full of just the nicest people. But it's only temporary. I suppose I have to get back to Washington at some point."

"Why?" Brooke asked. "You could stay here. We all did." She looked at Crystal. "Well, except her. She comes and goes like the wind."

Crystal smirked. "Ha. Funny. I happen to work in LA."

"But you don't have to. In fact, your boss would love it if you spent more time here," Alaina said sunnily before flashing her best friend a smile and then blowing her a kiss.

Crystal rolled her eyes.

"Now that I think about it, I guess I could do whatever I like," Gram said. "I've earned it, right? Maybe I will stay here." She looked over at Kelsey and winked. "Then I could be with my favorite girl."

Warmth spread through Kelsey's chest, and she hoped Gram decided to stay. How nice it would be to have family close by. Well, the *right* family. She shuddered to think of having her mother in the same town.

Darryl came back into the conference room and handed Alaina a list of archaeologists.

Her lips curved into her trademark thousand-watt smile. "Thanks, Darryl, we really appreciate it."

"You're welcome. I've got some work to do now, but stay as long as you like." He nodded before leaving the room.

Crystal held her hand out. "I'll call them."

Alaina handed her the paper. "Thanks."

"Let me talk to Luke Westcott first," Kelsey said. "Now that we know where the structure was located, I want to make sure we won't be disrupting any of their vines." She tried to picture where the homestead would be in terms of the present layout and couldn't really figure it out.

Crystal slipped the paper into her purse. "It may be that we need the archaeologist to come out and indicate where they need to work."

"Good point," Alaina said. She turned her head toward Kelsey. "But you're right about talking to the Westcotts and Hayden first. Let us know what they say."

"Sounds good." Crystal put her purse over her shoulder. "I'll make notes after I talk to each of them. Then we can decide as a group what to do next."

Alaina grinned. "See how efficient she is?"

They left the room and then the building, saying their good-byes outside. As Kelsey walked with Gram to the car, her phone pinged in her purse. She pulled it out and saw that it was Luke again, asking if she'd gotten his earlier text.

She responded, saying ten thirty was fine.

"Is that your not-date again?" Gram asked.

Kelsey fished around her purse for her keys. "Yes. And he *isn't* a date."

Gram sent her an unconvinced side-eye. "Mmm-hmm."

"*Really.*" Kelsey pulled out her keys.

"Maybe he should be," Gram said with a shrug.

Kelsey unlocked the car with her remote. "Gram."

"Sorry, I'll be quiet. I just want to see you happy again."

"I *am* happy. Especially now that you're here. I don't need a man in my life. You said so inside—just because Dorinda was alone doesn't mean she wasn't capable or successful. I'm both. As well as happy. Alone."

"You make an excellent argument. And you sound like me." She chuckled. "I can't find fault with that."

They got into the car, and Kelsey started up the engine. On the way back to Ribbon Ridge, she thought about Dorinda living the rest of her life alone after Hiram had died. Had that been her choice? Had she been happy? Kelsey hoped so.

Chapter Five

LUKE MADE THE very short drive to Kelsey's apartment and was fortunate to find an open spot to park at the curb. He shut the engine off and looked through the passenger window at the building. It was pre-1950, with businesses all along the ground floor. A hair-and-nail salon took up the most space on the corner. Next to it nestled a door that likely led up to Kelsey's apartment. He hadn't realized people still lived in the building.

He got out of the car and didn't even make it to the curb before she was already walking toward him with a brilliant, beautiful smile. Her hair was split into two dark, glossy braids that fell over each shoulder, and dark sunglasses covered her pale blue eyes. "Good morning! What a nice day for a hike. Though I hope it warms up a little." She rubbed her arms, which were covered in a violet-blue fleece pullover.

"It will." The sun was already shining, and the temperature would likely climb to the mid-seventies. Add in the exertion of hiking, and they'd be plenty warm. "I hope you're not too warm in jeans."

She glanced down before looking back at him, her dark brows arching elegantly over the top of her glasses. "Oh? Should I change? I see you have convertible pants on. I don't have any of those."

He knew he'd convert to shorts at some point. "Do you have anything lighter weight?"

"I might. It's just been a while since I did anything outdoorsy. Do you mind waiting while I go change?"

She wasn't going to invite him upstairs? "Sure."

"I'd invite you up, but my grandmother is staying with me, and she's in the middle of her morning routine." She flashed an apologetic smile. "Be right back."

Luke leaned against his car and waited maybe five minutes before she jogged back out the door in a lightweight pair of capris. She had great legs—long and lithe.

"Better?" she asked.

He nodded. "I think you'll be more comfortable. Ready?"

"Yep." She held up her hand, in which she clutched a hat. "And I almost forgot this. That would've been bad."

"For sure. But I keep extra caps in the car. I can't tell you how many times that's come in handy." He opened the door for her.

"Such a gentleman," she said softly.

"My mom would kill me if I wasn't." He closed the door with a smile and rounded the car—his trusty, beat-up, old Jeep—then climbed into the driver's seat. "It's about a thirty-minute drive. Do you like music or quiet?"

"Either is fine. I do so little driving anymore."

He fired up the engine and pulled onto Main Street, then took a quick right so he could loop back around and head west out of town.

"I guess that makes sense," he said. "You live and work in about a four-block radius, right?"

She chuckled. "Pretty much."

He slid her a glance. "Welcome to small-town life."

"I like it. I grew up in Chehalis, which isn't that much bigger."

"What brought you here to Ribbon Ridge?"

She took a moment to reply, and he sensed she was organizing what to say. Which made him wonder what she was censoring. "I was in a relationship, and he got a job in McMinnville. We lived there, but I worked at The Arch and Vine."

He remembered when she was new. That was a couple of years ago—when he and his brothers and Hayden had decided to buy the vineyard and start the winery. "I'm sorry things didn't work out for you with the relationship, but I'm glad you decided to stay in Ribbon Ridge."

"I really do love it. And I actually like being away from my family." She chuckled again. "Wow, that sounds terrible."

"Maybe," he said, smiling. "But your grandmother's here?"

"Oh yes, but she doesn't count. I adore her. I mean my mother. And my stepfather. Mostly my mother. We have a rather, um, tense relationship. Things are much better when there's distance between us."

"That sucks, but I get it. When I went to college in California, I was so happy to be away from my family—my mother, my father, my brothers, all of them." He glanced toward her and saw that she was watching him. "My introvertedness was at an all-time high then."

She nodded. "I so get you. I was thrilled to move to central Washington to go to college. I even graduated high school a year early."

He laughed. "Wow, you *were* desperate. And apparently very smart since you graduated early."

"I don't know if I'm particularly smart or just driven."

"I see. So when you go after something, everyone better move aside?"

She let out a sharp laugh. "I don't know about *that*."

"Well, I'll be keeping an eye on you." And that wouldn't be a hardship. They spent the rest of the trip talking about their college experiences and how they'd learned to come out of their shells a bit more. She mentioned that she'd been in a relationship, but he noticed she didn't say anything specific about it or the other person, which only doubled his curiosity. Or maybe it was nothing. It wasn't like he was telling her all about Paige and, really, there was *nothing* interesting there.

But it still accounted for three and a half years of his life. He inwardly flinched at how that sounded—that he'd spent three and a half years in a relationship that didn't bear mentioning. He pushed that from his mind as he turned into the parking area for the trailhead.

He parked near the large sign with a map of the area and turned the engine off. "I've got the packs in the back." He jumped out and went to the rear of his Jeep and opened the hatch.

She met him there, tugging her hat over her long braids.

He grabbed one of his caps from the Jeep and pulled it low on his head. Her hat was brimmed and made of khaki twill. It looked great on her. "You're clearly one of those women for whom hats are made."

"Guilty. I own at least two dozen. My favorites are winter hats, though. That's probably the bulk of my collection."

"Wow, that's impressive." He bet she looked

adorable in every single one of them. He pulled the hydration pack out of the Jeep and handed it to her. "This okay for you to wear?"

She pulled it on over her shoulders. "No problem."

"Cool. You know, I think I'm going to ditch the lower part of these pants right now." He unzipped the removable legs and tossed them into the Jeep. Then he tugged his pack on.

"Your backpack looks heavier," she said.

"Not much. It has a hydration chamber too, so think what you're wearing plus our lunch and some basic supplies. You know, in case we get into trouble." He locked the car and led her toward the trailhead.

"Uh-oh, what kind of trouble?"

He tightened the straps on his pack. "First aid, compass, water purification, extra food, that sort of thing."

She looked at him askance as they started on the trail. "You're the real deal."

He nodded. "Real enough, but not quite up to going out for more than a handful of days."

"Let me guess, only because you have to get back to work."

He laughed. "You know me so well already."

She threw him a flirty smile. "Like you said, it takes a workaholic to know one."

"Did I say that?" He couldn't resist flirting with her. He did wonder why she'd changed her mind about coming with him today and wanted to find a way to broach the subject.

The trail was wide enough for them to hike side by side. For now, at least. Once in a while, they'd have to go single file.

She adjusted her pack, tightening one of the straps.

"Oh, before I forget, I wanted to talk to you about the Bird's Nest Ranch."

At first he wasn't sure what that meant, but then remembered it was the historical structure that had been on the vineyard property. "I hope you aren't going to ask me to bulldoze my vines."

"Not at all. We were able to find where the house was located. Here." She stopped on the trail and pulled her phone from her back pocket. "I have a picture."

She tapped up the photo and then zoomed in so he could see it in better detail.

He took the phone and tried to figure out the placement of the house but had trouble finding his orientation. He zoomed back out, and that helped. "It looks like it's up on the ridge, right where Block D terminates. You might actually be able to find what you need without any disturbance." There was a space there between the pinot in Block D and the chardonnay in Block C. "It's hard to say, because the terrain may be different now if dirt's been moved around. The house would've been on a flat area, and what's there now doesn't seem large enough to support a house, but I guess it was probably fairly small."

"We'd like to hire an archaeologist to come out and survey. If you guys agree."

"Sure. Let me know when you want to set up a meeting. We'll have things we want to discuss with them first. I want to understand what they plan to do—how invasive they'll be. That sort of thing."

"Of course. Crystal is setting that up, but I'll make sure she gets in touch with you."

He handed the phone back to her. "Thanks."

"No, thank *you*." She stashed her phone in her pocket and gave him a warm smile. "We appreciate you being so cool about this."

It wasn't hard. He wanted to help. "What can I say, your passion for this project is contagious."

She laughed, and they continued along the trail for a few minutes.

He decided to pursue his curiosity about her. "So, uh, why'd you decide to come with me today?" He watched her body language to see if it would tell him anything.

She kept her gaze trained straight ahead. "My friends keep saying I should get out more, and they're right. And who better to get me away from work than another workaholic."

"I can't argue with your logic."

"So tell me about your family," she said, perhaps deflecting the topic to something safer. "You said you were happy to move to California, and yet you came back and started a business with your brothers. And don't you live with Jamie?"

"Uh, yeah." He adjusted his sunglasses over the bridge of his nose. "We'll see how much longer I can take it. I don't think I'm meant to have a roommate."

"I get you."

"But your grandma is staying with you. How's that going?"

"It's fine, to be honest. But she's moving out today. She's going to stay in an apartment at the Archers'."

"Over the garage," he said. "I'm familiar with it. Is she relocating to Ribbon Ridge?"

"She hasn't said, but I think she might be considering it. Can I tell you a secret?" She'd lowered her voice despite the fact that they were alone in the forest. "Maybe it isn't a secret, but it's sure...weird."

He slowed and angled toward her, anxious to hear

this now. "What?"

"When she first got here last week, she came to the pub, and she met George. They totally flirted with each other, and I'm pretty sure she's been over there to see him every day. Well, every day that he was there. He was gone once, and she was so disappointed. I think they might even be texting each other."

Luke howled with laughter. "How is that weird? That's *awesome*."

"Easy for you to say. She isn't your grandma!"

"No, but George is like everyone's grandpa. Or crazy uncle. Some sort of relative. He's quite beloved in Ribbon Ridge."

She sipped from the hydration pack. "Oh, believe me, I know. He's so nice to everyone, what's not to love? But he's different with my grandma. I think he *likes* her."

Luke couldn't help smiling. "God, I hope so. I'd love to see him settle down."

The trail narrowed for a few dozen yards, and Kelsey moved in front of him. "He's never been married?"

"Not that any of us know." Luke tried not to stare at her backside, but it was damned hard. Thankfully, no one could see him checking her out. "He was a strict military man for years—in the Marines. Then I think he was actually in some sort of intelligence position."

She glanced back over her shoulder, and he jerked his gaze up. "Wow. I didn't realize. He doesn't talk about that too much."

"No, he doesn't. He's pretty tight with Rob Archer, so I've heard a few things from Hayden." The trail widened again, and he quickened his pace to come abreast of her. "Now I'm going to be on the lookout for how George behaves next time I'm in the pub.

Maybe I'll ask him about his love life."

"No! You can't do that." She reached out and grabbed his forearm briefly. Her touch jolted through him like a rocket blasting off. Damn. "Forget I said anything."

"I wouldn't say anything," he said, his arm still thrumming from her touch.

"Hold up for a sec." She stopped and pulled the pack off, then set it at her feet, letting it lean against her ankle. Grasping the hem of her pullover, she whisked it up over her head. The garment tried to take her base layer—a pale blue tee—along with it, which exposed the slightly curved plane of her abdomen. Again, he tried not to fixate on her, but damn it was getting harder and harder.

Shit, *something* was getting harder.

He pivoted and willed his erection to stand the hell down. He hadn't been attracted like this to a woman since Paige. And their relationship had cooled considerably in the months leading to their breakup, so it had really been a long time.

When he chanced a glance back at Kelsey, she'd tied her fleece around her waist and was now pulling the pack back over her shoulders. "Ready," she said.

He started up the trail, and she fell in beside him. "So your grandmother might be moving here, maybe because of George. Do I have that right?" he asked.

"I don't know about the George part. We haven't discussed it. I suppose I should ask. I just didn't want to intrude. Relationships are just…personal."

Another thing they had in common. He recalled his conversation with his mother the other night. She seemed to want specific answers about why things hadn't worked out with Paige, but none of it was any of her business. Hell, he didn't like thinking about it, so why would he talk about it?

"I couldn't agree more," he said.

They walked down an embankment to the creek, an unnamed offshoot from the larger Gales Creek. "What a cute little bridge," she said.

He paused and waited for her to cross first—it was very small. "This was my brother's Eagle Scout project."

She turned when she reached the other side. "Really? That's so cool. What was yours?"

He walked across. "Also a bridge. On a different trail."

"Oh, you'll have to show me some time."

Really? "I'd love to. Maybe next Monday. We could make a habit out of this. At least as far as our jobs would allow."

She pivoted, and they continued along the trail. "I don't think I can do that. Definitely not next Monday. I'll need to catch up from playing hooky today."

"You should cut yourself some slack. The work will always be there." Had he really said that out loud? How many times had people told him the exact same thing and he'd told them to mind their own business? He winced. "Wow, that was an obnoxious thing to say." He reached out and offered her his hand. "Hi, Kettle? I'm Pot."

She laughed and took his hand. "Nice to meet you."

Again, the connection with her spread through him like an unchecked wildfire—hot and dangerous.

She pulled away from him, and her gaze trailed off. Had she felt that too? She busied herself with drinking from her pack.

Luke followed her lead and sucked back a bunch of

water. They walked on, falling silent for a few minutes. After a bit, she asked him if he had Netflix, and they embarked on a lengthy conversation about the ease of streaming programs and debated whether televisions were becoming obsolete.

Luke had a very large TV. "As long as there are televised sports, there will be televisions."

"And movies," she added. "Some movies are just no good on a smaller screen. Who wants to watch *The Avengers* on an iPad?"

"Very true." They reached the top of the rise, where the view of the surrounding countryside was gorgeous and they could even catch glimpses of Mt. Adams and Mt. St. Helens.

She turned a slow, complete circle. "This is so beautiful."

"One of my favorite views," he said, trying not to stare too hard at her. She was incredibly pretty. He wished she wasn't wearing her sunglasses so he could see the pale blue irises of her eyes. They reminded him of a babbling brook, where the water was clear and pristine.

He pulled his attention from her. "Ready to eat?"

"Sure."

He walked to a grassy patch, pulled off his pack, and sat down. "I hope you like turkey. I tried to go with something universal-ish."

She dropped to the grass beside him, and set her pack next to his. "What isn't universal? Just curious."

"I don't know…tuna, maybe?"

"Good point. I actually don't care for tuna sandwiches."

He handed her one of the sandwiches he'd made that morning. "Yay me."

She unwrapped the plastic. "Good choice of bread. This looks delicious." The sandwiches were on little baguettes with aioli, arugula, and swiss cheese.

"I have apples and some trail mix too."

"Sounds great. I'm starved."

He pulled the fruit and nuts from his pack and set them on the grass between them. They ate in silence for a few minutes.

After she finished off her turkey sandwich, she licked the edge of her mouth. It was incredibly erotic. Or maybe only to Luke, who'd somehow taken on the role of sex-starved lothario today. "You make a mean sandwich, Luke Westcott. Thank you."

She sipped from her water pack, and Luke decided he was far too fixated on her mouth. And every other part of her.

Get it together, man.

He'd finished his sandwich and downed a few handfuls of nuts before getting up. "I suppose we should head back." He checked his phone for the time. It was nearing one.

She got to her feet. "Sounds good. Ready when you are."

On the trip back, he focused on distracting topics, such as movies and books.

"I love that you read books," she said, smiling at him. "Sometimes I worry it's a lost art."

"And that's a librarian's worst nightmare, I'd imagine."

She laughed. "Actually, that's censorship. At least for me. So let's see, your favorite genre is outdoors or environmental nonfiction. Do you read any fiction?"

"Sure. I like spy thrillers. And some speculative fiction. I got a little burned out on that, though. Lately,

I've started reading historical fiction."

"I'd be happy to recommend some titles when you come by the library."

The trail narrowed a bit, and the surrounding foliage was thick. "Thanks, I'd really appreciate that. I'll be sure to stop in soon."

She looked over at him and didn't see the branch until it smacked her in the eye.

Luke hadn't seen it either because his attention was too focused on her instead of their surroundings. He also wasn't fast enough to catch her before she fell.

ॐ

THE STINGING PAIN brought tears to Kelsey's eyes as her knees buckled. She shouldn't have fallen over at all, but she'd been hit too many times, and her reflex was to ball herself up. Not that she did that exactly; she just ended up on her butt.

Luke immediately dropped down beside her. "Are you okay?"

She blinked, but the pain was still there. The branch had snapped against her left eye—the side that had always taken the most abuse. "I'll be fine."

How many times had she told herself that? She took a deep breath, held it for a count of three, and slowly let it out. How many times had she done that too?

"Hey, you're bleeding a little." He shrugged out of his backpack and brought it around to unzip the main pocket. He drew out a first aid kit and found a piece of gauze that he dabbed against her brow, just above her eye.

She couldn't stop herself from flinching. *He's trying to*

help you, she reminded herself.

"Yikes, that really hurts, doesn't it? I'm so sorry, Kelsey."

"It's not your fault." Those words tasted so damn bitter on her tongue, which was stupid because in this case it *hadn't* been his fault. Goddammit, had Noah absolutely ruined her?

She already knew the answer to that.

"I wish I had some ice to put on that," he said. He stared at her with such care, his brow creased, his brown eyes tinged with concern. Close up, she could see the fine stubble along his jaw. She'd never seen him quite clean-shaven, which she found incredibly sexy.

"It's all right, I'm good." She tried to stand, but he reached out and took her hand, then pulled her down.

"Let's just sit for a minute. Let you regain your equilibrium. And then I can put a bandage on this."

"That's not necessary."

"Come on, I have a whole first aid kit I barely ever use. Please let me use a bandage?"

A smile crept over her, and she relaxed.

He plucked some antibacterial spray from the kit and removed the gauze he'd been holding against her. "Looks like it stopped bleeding." He sprayed the wound and put the medicine away, then withdrew a bandage, which he tried to open and failed. "Who the hell designed these wrappers?"

She took it from him, her fingers grazing his. "Let me."

She tore it open—it wasn't easy—and handed it back to him.

"Excellent. Remind me to call you when I can't open the pickle jar either."

She smiled again, loving his sense of humor and how

comfortable he made her feel.

He placed the bandage against the wound and glided his fingertips over it to smooth the adhesive against her. "There. All better." His hand lingered, his fingers stroking her forehead and temple.

She couldn't look away from his mesmerizing gaze— it was intense but also calming. Then his eyes narrowed, and his fingers brushed along her hairline. "Ouch, what's this scar from?"

Oh shit. She'd been so caught up in the moment that she'd forgotten that was there. And with her hair pulled back into a braid, it was far more noticeable than when her hair was loose. She had a rehearsed excuse, but it froze on her tongue. The words that came out instead shocked the hell out of her.

"My ex broke a beer bottle over my head."

His gaze widened, mirroring her own surprise. What the hell had she just done?

"God, Kelsey," he breathed, his voice low and dark. "Where is that son of a bitch now?"

"Prison. Thankfully."

"Good, because if I ever see him, I might have to return the favor. Or worse." The brown of his eyes turned nearly black, and a wave of anxiety crested over her. She appreciated his sentiment, but if he was the type of guy that resorted to violence, she didn't want any part of him. Not even as a friend.

She backed away and was glad that he let her. Standing, she brushed her hands against her thighs. "Thanks, uh, for taking care of that."

He put the bandage wrapper and the first aid kit into the backpack and zipped it up. He moved slowly, and she could practically hear the gears of his mind turning. Why on earth had she told him that? She didn't talk about Noah or his abuse. Not outside of reporting it to the police and begrudgingly telling her family why they'd broken up. She'd considered hiding it from them too—God, it was beyond humiliating—but had ultimately spilled the beans. What a mistake that had been, given her mother's characteristically unsympathetic response.

He pulled the backpack over his shoulders and looked at her, his lips pressed together. "Kelsey—"

"Can we forget I said anything? We were having such a nice day." She just wanted to get back to the car. And then spend thirty minutes driving back with him. Ugh, what a disaster.

"No, we can't. That's a big deal." He pulled his hat off and ran his free hand through his hair. "But we don't have to talk about it if you don't want to. If you ever do, I'd be happy to listen. No, it would be my privilege to listen." The darkness had gone from his gaze and was replaced with a simple sincerity and warmth that made her breath hitch.

"Thank you. I appreciate that more than you can know."

He put his hat back on and nodded. "Okay then, should we continue?"

"Absolutely."

The conversation was intermittent at best until they were almost back to the car. "I'm sorry if I ruined the hike," she said.

His head swung toward her. "Not at all. I was just thinking what a great time I had. You're a terrific hike partner. We've done almost six miles, and you haven't slowed a bit. Even after taking a branch to the face."

"Is it bad if I admit that I'm glad we're almost back?"

He chuckled. "Not at all. I respect your honesty. You

know, that bandage makes you look rather dashing—not quite a pirate, but definitely bordering on badass."

"Thanks. I think."

"I definitely meant it as a compliment." They emerged from the trail into the parking lot. "And here we are." He unlocked the car and opened the back.

"That was great. Thanks again for inviting me."

He took a long drink from his pack before pulling it off and tossing it into the Jeep. "Thanks for coming. I hope you'll hike with me again some time."

She took off her pack and set it in the car. "I'd like that."

"Great." He sat on the bumper. "So, this coming weekend is the Ribbon Ridge Oktoberfest. Have you been before?"

She nodded, tensing for what might come next. And she was right.

"Would you like to go with me? Whenever you can fit it into your schedule."

She did have Saturday evening off. She could say yes. But that didn't mean she should. Today had been fun, but after telling Luke about Noah... She wanted to crawl into a hole and bury her head for a week. Or forever.

"I'm actually really booked up this weekend. Two jobs and all that."

He turned his head away from her slightly and looked out toward the road. "Right. I get that. Well, if you change your mind, or your schedule frees up, let me know."

He sounded disappointed. She actually felt a little disappointed, but it was for the best. There'd been a moment—okay, several moments—when she'd felt so comfortable with him...so *drawn* to him. How else could she explain telling him about Noah? She'd never done that and even now couldn't quite understand *why* she'd done it. Had she known that he would be so supportive? He hadn't pressed her in the slightest, and that gave her something she hadn't felt in a long time: hope.

For what? A relationship? She tried to imagine how that would work. She hadn't even been able to handle him tending her wound without shrinking away. What would happen when he kissed her or touched her…intimately? The last year or so with Noah had been so awful.

Yep, she was ruined. Her heart ached.

Luke stood up from the bumper. "You ready?"

She sensed his impatience. Or frustration. Or both. "Yep." She moved away from the back end and went to the passenger door as he shut the hatch.

Once they were in the Jeep, he fired up the engine and pulled out of the lot.

After five minutes or so, he yanked his hat off and tossed it into the backseat, then ran his hand through his hair, making it stand up. It gave him a just-rolled-out-of-bed look that was far sexier than it ought to be. Kelsey tried to ignore the visceral reaction burgeoning in her gut. She hadn't been attracted to someone in so long. The sensation was a bit frightening.

"Any chance you want to tell me about your ex?" he asked, keeping his gaze on the road. "Nothing major. How long were you together?"

She *didn't* want to tell him. She kept hoping that chapter in her life would just miraculously disappear. Hence the reason she never talked about it. Maybe if she didn't, she could pretend it had never happened. Except things like the scar he'd noticed would always be there to remind her. And someday, Noah would get out of prison, and she'd have to deal with that. Her stomach knotted.

"We met in college. We were together about six years."

That sounded so awful. How could she not have known better?

"I imagine you had some happy times."

The knot in her stomach vaulted to her throat. How could he know that? How did he know just the right thing to say to ease the tension curdling through her? "We did."

Until she'd gone to grad school in Seattle. He'd come with her and hated every minute of living in the urban environment. He'd hit her a few times in college, but things had worsened in Seattle. It had started with him throwing things, followed by putting his fist through the wall. He'd progressed to shoving her or grabbing her hard enough to leave bruises and on to slapping and occasionally closed-fist punching. Then the hitting had become more regular, but still not bad enough for her to realize what was happening. At the time, at least. In retrospect, she'd been an idiot.

He'd saved his grand performance—beating the crap out of her—for when they'd moved far away from family. From his comfort zone. In small-town Oregon, he'd been able to isolate her, to ensure that he was her sole relationship. And she'd fallen into that trap like an idiot. She clasped her hands in her lap and squeezed as her agitation built.

"How'd he end up in prison? I mean, did you have a trial and all that?"

She would've, if it had been necessary, but Noah had taken the plea deal. "He pled guilty to assault."

"I'm glad you didn't have to go through a trial. Not after everything else."

He had no idea what she'd been through. He was making assumptions. And yet, he was absolutely right. And he got it. Or seemed to anyway. She didn't know what to do with that.

She shifted in her seat. "I'm sorry, but can we talk about something else?"

"Of course. I'm sorry. I'm just… I'm upset. Which is dumb, I guess."

"It isn't." She'd so wanted someone to respond this way when it had happened, but she hadn't had any friends—Noah had done a great job of isolating her from everyone. And her mother had blamed her. Gram would've been there for her, but Grandpa had just died, and Kelsey hadn't wanted to burden her. "I appreciate your concern. Truly. But I like to leave it in the past where it belongs."

"I get that. Do you mind my asking when this happened?"

"About two years ago." She remembered that night so vividly. Summer had just turned to fall, and she'd been so looking forward to the holiday season. They'd started talking about marriage, and she'd been certain he would propose. Now she knew she'd dodged a bullet.

"That was here, then," he said. "In Ribbon Ridge. I remember meeting you at least two years ago."

"Yes." They'd been living in the area maybe three or four months. She angled herself away from him and focused out the passenger-side window, hoping he'd drop the subject.

"Damn, I keep talking about it, sorry. I'm a dick." He exhaled. "So, I had a girlfriend before." He let out a sharp laugh. "That sounded stupid. I had a girlfriend in California. We tried a long-distance thing when I moved back here, but it didn't work out."

She turned back toward him, grateful for the change in topic. The fact that he was offering up his own love life for discussion intrigued her. "Was it because the relationship was long distance, or was it doomed before that?"

He slid her a glance tinged with admiration. "You're very astute. It wasn't great. I think I knew that. Hell, it was probably part of why I decided to come back."

"Ouch. That's pretty telling if you have to move to another state."

"Yeah, I guess. Wait, that's not fair. Paige is a nice person. I still like her, actually." He sounded a bit confused. Or surprised. Like he hadn't expected to say that.

Kelsey couldn't imagine a conciliatory breakup. "That's nice. You're lucky."

They were nearing Ribbon Ridge, and Kelsey looked forward to getting home, jumping in the shower, and being alone. Except she'd told Gram she'd drop by her new apartment after the hike. Kelsey had offered to cancel and help, but Gram had *insisted* she keep her "date."

Kelsey looked over at Luke. His profile was devilishly handsome with his sexy stubble and the firm line of his jaw. "Luke?"

He flicked her a glance. "Yeah?"

"Was today a date?"

"Uh. I sort of thought so, but I'm not really sure. Does it matter?"

It was what it was, right? She'd had a good time. Until she'd messed it up. "I guess not. I just wanted to, you know, understand your expectations. You know what, never mind. I had a good time, and that's all that matters."

He nodded firmly. "Absolutely."

They were quiet until he pulled into Ribbon Ridge. "Are you going to work after I drop you off?" he asked.

It was nearing four. She had plenty of time to go to the library and get a couple of hours in, but no, she'd go visit Gram. She looked at him askance. "No. Are you?"

"Ha! Maybe. We'll see how I feel after I shower. I'm sure I have plenty of e-mail from Cam to read. He's busy coordinating our first wine club dinner in a couple of weeks, and he's adamant that we all chime in. But really, what the hell do I know about planning an event?"

"Probably more than you realize. I mean, you know what you like, right?"

His gaze shot toward her and lingered. "I do."

Heat pooled in her belly, and she wondered if she ought to let her guard down. He was pretty great. But the nagging fear that he could be someone entirely different from what he presented was nearly crippling.

She didn't respond because she couldn't think of a thing to say. He pulled onto Main Street and got into the right lane. There weren't any open parking spots in front of her building, so he had to turn the corner.

"You can just drop me here," she said.

He slowed the car. "Are you sure?"

"Yeah, it's no problem."

He pulled into an empty loading zone. "It's also not very gentlemanly of me to let you out around the block from your apartment. I wanted to park and walk you to your door."

Like a date. "It's fine. I'll talk to you soon—thanks again." She flashed him a smile and jumped out of the Jeep.

"I had a great time." His gaze found hers. "See you soon, I hope."

Yeah, don't count on that. Except it was hard to avoid people in Ribbon Ridge, especially if someone wanted to run into you—as apparently he did—but she'd do her best.

She waved before closing the door and heading to her apartment. She climbed the stairs and unlocked the door, then stopped as she realized it was empty again. Gram had only been here a short time, but Kelsey suddenly felt very alone. It had never bothered her before. In fact, she'd been thrilled to have her own space for the first time since she was eighteen and in her second year of college.

Tossing her hat on the couch, she made her way into the small kitchen. This morning's dishes were stacked neatly in the drying rack, despite her telling Gram that she should leave them.

Yep, she was going to miss having Gram as a roommate.

She texted Gram to let her know that she was home. Gram responded with an invitation to join her at the Archers' for a salmon bake. Rob and Emily, who owned the apartment and lived in the house where it was located, had insisted on making her a welcome dinner, and she wanted Kelsey to come too.

After the way today had ended, Kelsey wasn't sure she wanted to mingle with people she didn't know very well. It was amazing—and frustrating—how raw she could still feel. Screw that. Noah wasn't going to control her anymore. She'd go to the damn dinner, and she'd have a great time.

Although she felt proud of her outlook, a tiny voice in the back of her head asked why she couldn't take that tack with Luke.

Because she was scared to death.

Chapter Six

AFTER SPENDING THE morning in the vineyard, Luke sat at his desk to eat a sandwich. He fired up his laptop and scanned his e-mail. Disappointment nagged at his insides. What had he been hoping for? That Kelsey would e-mail him because she'd somehow forgotten how to text?

He wasn't surprised given how shaken she'd been yesterday. He still couldn't quite process what she'd told him, which had been damn little. He wanted to know everything about this abusive asshole and ensure he could never hurt her again.

Which is why he's in prison, dick-for-brains.

But for how long? It wasn't as if domestic violence would give him a life sentence. No, those fuckheads usually got out long before they should. And in many cases, they never went to jail at all.

His office phone rang, and he immediately picked up the receiver without looking at the caller ID. "West Arch, this is Luke."

"Hey, Luke." The voice was feminine, but not the one he wanted to hear.

"Paige. Hi." He sat back in his chair and briefly closed his eyes. That'd teach him to answer without checking the caller ID.

"It's been a while," she said. "How are you?"

"Great. Just finished the harvest. Busy, busy."

"Right. How's it going up there? I remember it being

gorgeous in the fall."

She'd come up to visit several times after he'd moved back—when they'd tried to maintain their relationship long distance. In hindsight, he'd known it wouldn't work. Rather, that he'd wanted out. But he'd let the distance do the breaking up for him. Shit, was he that big of a jerk?

He sat up and scooted his chair toward his desk. Paige was a nice person, and when he'd told her they could be friends, he'd meant it. He'd never wanted to hurt her. Which was perhaps why he hadn't handled things well. He'd hoped she would be the one to break things off. But that plan had failed. "It's going well, thanks. How are things with you? Still liking Westerly?"

"No, actually. I got laid off last month."

"Wow, I'm sorry to hear that. But you're great at what you do, and you're in the right area to find something relatively quickly."

"It looks that way on paper, but I haven't found anything yet." She sounded frustrated, and he felt bad for her. "I've actually been looking up in your area. Will you let me know if you hear of anything?"

She was an event planner and had managed the cellar club at Westerly Estate. Before that, they'd worked at the same winery where she'd done the same job. The owner hadn't liked them seeing each other and because he didn't want to lose his vineyard manager, he'd let her go. Luke had felt terrible, and he'd pulled some strings to get her on at Westerly. Not that it had been tough because she was great at what she did. But networking was huge in their industry.

"Um, yeah, I'll keep an eye out."

"I don't suppose your winery is hiring." She laughed. "That wouldn't be weird, would it?"

Maybe not weird, but definitely awkward as hell. "We can't afford you." That was true. They couldn't really afford any additional staff right now. As far as he knew. He left that to Jamie and Cam. And he wasn't going to ask. He didn't mind helping her out, but she couldn't work here.

"I'll take that as a compliment," she said. "So are you seeing anyone now?"

She'd never been one to mince words. He'd liked that about her. He thought of Kelsey and wanted to say yes, but he couldn't. Not in good conscience. "Not really."

"Interesting." She strung the word out a bit. "That's not a firm no. So maybe there *is* someone."

He smiled and shook his head. "No, there really isn't." Even if there was, he wouldn't talk about her with his ex. "Listen, I need to get back to things here. It's good to hear from you."

"It's good to talk to you. I still miss you. Sorry, I can't help it." She exhaled. "Anyway, if you hear of anything that might work for me up there, will you let me know? I really need a job."

He felt for her. Truly. And he would see what he could find—maybe in the southern valley so she wasn't too close. "Definitely."

"Thanks, Luke. Keep in touch, okay?"

Cam and Jamie appeared at the threshold to his office and stalked inside, each taking a chair near the windows that looked out over the vineyard. Luke angled himself away from them to finish the call. "Sure thing. Talk to you later. Bye, Paige." He hung up and swung back around.

Jamie's brows climbed his forehead. "Paige?"

"Yep. What do you guys need?" He could see from

their exchanged look that he was not going to dodge the Paige conversation.

"What did she want?" Cam asked.

"Just checking in. She's looking for a job and wanted to know if I knew of anything up here."

Cam set his elbow on the armrest. "Well, that wouldn't be awkward."

"Not at all," Jamie said. "What did you tell her?"

Luke shrugged. "I said I'd keep an eye out. Maybe in the southern valley."

Cam smiled. "Good call."

"She asked if we were hiring—now *that* would be awkward. Thankfully, I didn't have to lie."

"Actually, that's why we're here," Cam said, exchanging another look with Jamie. "Juggling this cellar club along with everything else is just proving too much. And sales are going much better than we anticipated."

Luke grinned at them. "Great problem to have."

Jamie nodded. "For sure. I've crunched some numbers, and we can afford to take on an employee to help with sales and manage the cellar club as well as plan events."

Damn, that sounded right up Paige's alley. If they advertised this job, she'd apply in a heartbeat.

Cam chuckled. "I can see the fear in your eyes, brother. Don't worry, we already have someone in mind, and I know she'll take the position."

Luke had a suspicion he knew who this was, but asked anyway. "Who's that?"

"Brooke," Cam said. "She's more than qualified."

"And she can put up with you that much?" Luke teased.

"So she says."

"Maybe she'll keep him in line," Jamie said, winking at Luke.

Cam rolled his eyes. "Like I need that. You guys are tools. I've talked to her about it, and she's totally on board."

"You talked to her first?" Luke asked. This was *their* business.

"Only to see if she was even interested. I made it clear that it wasn't a job offer—that we hadn't discussed it yet."

Luke appreciated that. And, really, he shouldn't have doubted his brother. "Hayden should be in on this too."

"Definitely," Jamie said. "We stopped in and asked him to join us, but he's up to his eyeballs in grapes right now. He said he'd come up when he could."

"Well, I have no problem with bringing Brooke on. She's sure sold a shit ton of our wine." They'd contracted her as their distributor last summer, and she'd done a bang-up job. In fact, she was the reason their cellar club had taken off so well. He looked at Jamie. "As long as you say we can afford it."

Jamie gripped the arms of the chair. "We can."

Luke cast Cam a skeptical look. "And you're sure you don't mind working with your wife? That's a lot of together time." That sounded hellish to Luke. He'd hated that Paige had lost her job after they'd started dating, but he'd also been relieved not to spend so much time together.

"Not at all," Cam said, his eyes taking on a blissful sheen. "I'd spend every moment with her if I could."

Luke blinked and then looked at Jamie, who promptly made a gagging motion, jabbing his finger into his mouth. Luke laughed, and Cam reached over and socked Jamie in the arm.

"You guys are just jealous," Cam said.

"Nah." *Maybe,* a rebellious voice clamored in the recesses of Luke's brain. He ignored it. "I like my space too much."

"Yeah, about that," Jamie said slowly.

Luke leaned forward, suddenly very alert. And expectant. And maybe a wee bit excited.

Jamie turned toward Cam. "Any chance Brooke is giving notice at the lofts? I'd kind of like my own digs." He jerked his head toward Luke. "No offense, bro. Our situation is great and was super helpful after we sank all this money into buying the vineyard."

"None taken." Luke felt as though something that had been coiled tight inside him was beginning to unfurl.

"Actually, Brooke did give notice just yesterday," Cam said. "She thought she knew someone who might want it, but it turns out they don't."

Jamie grinned. "Excellent. I'll contact the property manager and submit an application. Hopefully beat anybody else to the punch." He looked back to Luke. "You okay with that?"

"Yeah." More than okay. He was ecstatic. "How soon do you think you'll move?"

Cam laughed. "Can't wait to get rid of him, eh? I can't blame you. He's always been the messy one."

"Hey. I'm cleaner now," Jamie protested.

"Not much," Luke stage-whispered toward Cam.

Jamie snorted and jumped to his feet. "I'm going to call the manager now. Catch you losers later."

"Good talk," Cam yelled after him as he left. He turned his head back to look at Luke. "How was your hike yesterday?"

Luke hadn't mentioned that he'd gone with Kelsey and decided not to say anything now. Not after what had happened. Not since he doubted there'd be a repeat, though he hoped he was wrong.

"It was good. Just an out and back at Gales Creek."

"I bet it felt great to have a day to yourself. You more than deserve it."

Luke appreciated the sentiment. He was surprised at how much he enjoyed working with his brothers. He'd been a little nervous about it at first, because he did enjoy his autonomy so much, but things had turned out well so far. "Thanks. You deserve some time off too. Maybe with Brooke joining the team, you'll be able to do that."

"That's the idea. I need more time to spend with my future wife—we have wedding planning to do, apparently."

Luke laughed. "Well, you'll be spending a lot more time with her."

"Yes, but I mean nonwork related. I just need to get through the cellar club dinner and then we can focus on wedding plans."

"You pick a date yet?"

"Not yet. That's something else I need to talk to you guys about. We'd like to get married in the vineyard and have the reception here."

For some odd and very stupid reason, Luke felt a burn of envy. He was very proprietary about his vineyard, and it just felt like if someone was going to get married in it, that person should be him. Which was ridiculous. "I have no problem with that. Makes sense, really."

Cam exhaled. "I'm so glad you feel that way. I was concerned you wouldn't want us messing with the vineyard. Actually, I see us getting married closer to the winery here, really with the vineyard in the background. We're looking at dates in June."

"Weather's tricky in June," Luke said. "But we'll have a few more tents by then." Part of their long-term planning involved adding a few tents every year as their events grew over time. They planned on hosting dinners in the vineyard and during certain times of the year, Oregon weather could be unreliable.

"Yeah, that's my thought. We talked about August, but I think we'd rather get married sooner than later." His eyes took on a far-off look—that blissed-out expression again. "That's what happens when you find The One. You can't wait to start your life together. Which we already have, really."

"I think it's great." Luke was really happy for his brother, particularly after the heartache he'd endured.

"Thanks, bro." Cam stood. "I'm going to go talk to Hayden about Brooke, since he didn't make his way up here."

"Good plan. Catch you later."

Cam waved as he left, and Luke went back to finishing his sandwich. Damn, he was going to have his own place again! He could hardly wait.

And yet, he was surprisingly envious of Cam and his happiness with Brooke. Luke had never seen his brother so full of joy and peace.

His mind turned to Kelsey again, and he promptly told himself to knock it off. She'd tried to dissuade him when he'd asked her out. *But then she'd changed her mind,* he reminded himself. Her nonverbals yesterday had told him all he really needed to know—she still wasn't over her last relationship. Not that he could blame her. He wished the timing were different, because he really liked her.

Damn.

♥️

WEDNESDAYS WERE THE only day Kelsey worked a full eight-hour shift at the pub, because the library was closed. It meant she was able to take a whopping half-hour lunch break, which had just started. She carried her favorite salad—and a Diet Coke—to the table in the corner.

George called out to her. "I see you remembered your drink for once."

"I did, thanks, George." She chuckled to herself as she sat down.

A few minutes later, she looked up, thinking she heard Gram's voice. And she had—there she was, talking to George at the bar. They stood in profile, but Kelsey could see their expressions. They were both grinning, their eyes dancing in open flirtation. It would be disgusting if it wasn't so adorable. Wow, had Gram just giggled?

At last, their heads turned as George nodded toward Kelsey. Gram gave him a last coquettish smile as she turned.

Kelsey sipped her Diet Coke and noticed Gram was carrying a brown paper bag with handles. "I see you and George are getting along famously."

Gram blushed as she sat down opposite Kelsey. "Yes. He just asked me out." Her eyes widened, and she giggled again. "I wasn't sure what to say."

Kelsey leaned forward. "What *did* you say?"

Gram shrugged. "I said yes. We're going to the

Oktoberfest on Saturday night. He says it's quite the event."

"It is. Great food, music, and, of course, beer. The Archers sponsor it."

"Yes, Emily mentioned it this morning." Gram gave her a pointed look. "That woman makes the best crockpot oatmeal."

Kelsey let out a laugh. "Sounds like you're fitting right in here."

"Yes, in fact, I think I'm going to stay. Well, I guess I have to since I just accepted a job."

Kelsey had picked up her fork and nearly dropped it into her salad. "You what? Why do you need a job?" She didn't remember Gram working. Maybe ever.

"I realized I needed something to do when I was still living with your mother. I'm bored, dear. Maybe if you got married and gave me some great-grandchildren, I'd have something to do!" She laughed, and Kelsey just shook her head, smiling. Gram understood why Kelsey was single—at least Kelsey thought she did. They'd talked about it briefly since she'd come to town, and Gram hadn't pressed her when she'd said she just liked being on her own.

"So what's the job?" Kelsey asked before digging back into her salad.

"I'll be working at The Knitty Gritty just down the block."

Kelsey loved that store, even though she didn't knit. They had a variety of stuff from home décor to paper goods to funny gifts. They also sold yarn and knitting supplies. "Gram, you don't knit."

"I know, it's crazy, isn't it?" She picked up the bag she'd set next to her chair. "I bought some yarn and needles and a book. The owner said she'd give me a

So Right

lesson tomorrow."

Kelsey sipped her Diet Coke to wash down her last bite. "So in one day, you've picked up a job, a hobby, and a date. I think you've more than solved your boredom."

Gram laughed. "Isn't it marvelous?"

Yes, it was. Kelsey loved seeing Gram this animated. She just loved seeing Gram period. "I'm so glad you've decided to stay. Have you told Mom?"

Gram's expression dimmed. "Not yet. She'll say it's a mistake."

Kelsey made a sound of disgust. "Who cares? She thinks everything that isn't her idea is a mistake."

"True. She'll try to talk me out of it."

"Can she?"

Gram reached across the table and clasped Kelsey's hand. "No. I'm here to stay, whether you like it or not. I just need somewhere to live. I was thinking I might try to find a little place outside of town. Maybe on an acre or two so I can have some animals. Then you can come live with me and get out of that awful apartment."

"It's not so bad."

Gram pursed her lips. "It has no dishwasher, the tub barely drains, and the pipes are so loud, they'd wake the dead."

Kelsey couldn't dispute any of that. It was strange, but after having Gram with her for a few days, it was as though she was seeing the apartment through new eyes. She'd begun to think she should've taken Brooke up on the loft vacancy. Yes, it was expensive, and it meant she couldn't pay off her loans as quickly as she'd like, but maybe that was worth having comfort? Brooke's loft had a sumptuous bathroom. When Kelsey thought of curling up with a book in a steaming bath, she could hardly keep from sighing in anticipation.

Yeah, maybe she should talk to Brooke about that.

"Okay, so my apartment sucks. But you don't want to live with me. I'd cramp your style." Kelsey nodded toward George, who just happened to be looking their way. He smiled and raised his hand to acknowledge her. Kelsey lifted her glass in silent toast.

Gram's eyes widened again. "What are you doing?"

"I think George knows we're talking about him."

Gram shook her head. "But we aren't."

"We were, and we will again. Like I said, I'd cramp your style. How can you have George over with me hanging about?"

"I, uh… I don't know. It doesn't matter. You're lovely to have around."

"Not if you're trying to be romantic. What if you want to have a sleepover?"

"Kelsey!" Gram looked shocked for a moment, and then she laughed, her cheeks turning pink. "We'll go to his house."

"Ha! So you've thought about it."

"Maybe." Gram's cheeks grew red. "Anyway, I'll talk to the Archers about house hunting. They'll point me in the right direction."

Kelsey sat back in her chair and crossed her arms, grinning. She was absurdly delighted with Gram and George. She just hoped it—whatever "it" was— worked out. "Yep."

George walked toward the table then. "Here he comes," Kelsey whispered.

Gram sat straighter and smoothed her hands over her cheeks as the last of the pink faded away.

He came to a stop and looked down at Gram.

"Forgive me, but I forgot to ask what you wanted to drink? Can I get you a shandy?"

That was Gram's favorite drink—beer and lemonade. At least that was her version of a shandy, and Kelsey had to assume that George had already learned to make it to her taste, since he seemed to know it was her favorite.

She smiled up at him, looking ten years younger. "Yes, thank you."

He nodded before taking off, and Kelsey felt a surprising twinge of envy. She remembered that feeling of fresh attraction, of new emotions, of the prospect of joy. She realized she'd felt a jolt of that the other day with Luke when he'd tended to her wound. Before she'd mucked everything up by mentioning stupid Noah. Her pulse had quickened, and she'd wanted to lose herself in his eyes. She hadn't thought that was possible anymore. And maybe it wasn't. But for a brief, fleeting moment, it had seemed within reach. If only she had the courage to grab it.

She wasn't sure she did.

George returned with the shandy, and they chatted for a few minutes before he reluctantly went back to the bar. Gram watched him go with a wistful look in her eyes.

"You two are too cute," Kelsey said. "I'm afraid I have to get back to work soon, and I need to run home for a few minutes." She needed to throw a chicken breast in her mini-crockpot for dinner.

Gram stood. "I guess I'll go try to figure out how to knit. After I finish my shandy at the bar." She winked at Kelsey as she picked up her bag and drink and went to join George.

Kelsey bussed her dishes to the kitchen and waved at

Gram and George as she walked by on her way outside.

Their stunning fall weather had dimmed a bit today as the clouds had moved in. It was supposed to rain tomorrow for the start of Oktoberfest, but the forecasters were sure it would clear up on Friday. As sure as forecasters could be anyway.

Kelsey crossed the street and took care of her dinner prep. Then, on her way out of the building, she came face-to-face with Luke Westcott.

They both stopped short, and she imagined her face reflected the surprise on his.

"Fancy meeting you here," he said, grinning.

She wasn't sure what she'd expected when she saw him again, but she was relieved that it wasn't awkward. One of the reasons she didn't tell people about her past with Noah was that she didn't want them treating her with kid gloves. She hated feeling like a victim. So far, Luke hadn't made her feel like that.

"Yes, fancy that," she said. "Since I *live* here." She smiled at him.

"Okay, you caught me. I actually hoped I'd run into you. In fact, I was on my way to The Arch and Vine."

Somehow, the spontaneity of their meeting had made it seem…safer. Which was stupid. He wasn't unsafe. What the hell was wrong with her?

A guy's interested in you, and you're paralyzed. Duh. That's what's wrong with you.

"You were?"

He nodded. "I just…I've been thinking about you a lot since Monday, and I just… Wow, my speaking skills are really stellar here." He rubbed his hand along his unshaven jaw.

She laughed. "You're fine."

"Well, I just wanted you to know. That I was

thinking of you. That I hope we're friends. I really would like to be."

Men and women could be friends of course. It was just that Kelsey didn't have any guy friends. She thought of the men she worked with—George, Mick, and the others. She supposed they were friends. But maybe not. It wasn't as if she did things with them outside work. Until she and Brooke had become friends, she hadn't done anything with anyone outside work.

The courage she'd been hoping for a little while ago gathered inside her. "I was thinking I might want to go to Oktoberfest after all. I'll tag along with you, if you don't mind."

He didn't immediately answer, and she held her breath. His brow furrowed slightly and he stared at her a moment. "Okay, that's twice now I've asked you out and you've declined only to change your mind. Is this how you do things? Because it's a bit demoralizing."

Ouch. She deserved that. "No, it's not how I do things. Honestly, I'm terribly out of practice. Forget I said anything. You should probably run in the other direction."

He lightly touched her forearm and guided her toward the building. She realized someone needed to walk by, and they were sort of hogging the sidewalk.

His gaze was steady and warm as he looked at her. "I don't want to run the other way. I want to take you to Oktoberfest. On a date. Just so we're clear."

A date. That sensation of wanting to fall into his eyes stole over her again. This time, she didn't shrink away. "Okay."

His lips curved into a handsome smile. "Okay. I'll pick you up at six, if that works."

"Yep, that's great. See you then." Neither one of them moved for a moment. "I need to get back to work. My lunch is over."

"Oh. Well, I'll walk with you since I'd planned to pick up lunch anyway."

They crossed the street, and when they reached the other side, she turned to look at him. "You can meet my grandmother. She's inside flirting with George."

He grinned. "That sounds fantastic. I can't wait to give George a hard time."

She elbowed him as they approached the door. "Be nice. They're very cute."

"I bet. I was only teasing. I'm happy for them both."

"He's taking her to Oktoberfest on Saturday too."

He opened the door for her. "Should we double-date?"

"God, no." She slapped her hand over her mouth. "Well, that sounded terrible." She laughed. "I only meant that I don't want to intrude on them. But it was nice of you to offer."

"In all honesty, now that I finally get to take you on a date, I don't really want to share you either."

A giddy heat skipped through her. Gram was still seated at the bar, though her shandy glass was empty.

George's gaze flicked over them. "What did you drag in with you, Kelsey?"

Luke laughed, and Kelsey shook her head. Gram turned on the stool and surveyed Luke intently.

"Gram, this is Luke Westcott," Kelsey said. "I went hiking with him the other day."

Gram nodded. "This is the young man." She held out her hand. "I'm pleased to meet you, Luke. Call me Ruby."

He shook her hand. "A beautiful stone for a

beautiful woman."

Gram chuckled, and she gave Kelsey an approving nod. "Aren't you delightful?"

Later, Kelsey would caution Gram not to get too excited. She'd agreed to a date and nothing more. And even now she began to wonder if she'd been too hasty.

Don't be ridiculous. Luke's a nice guy, and you are more than ready for a date.

She told herself to breathe.

"Back off, Westcott," George barked. "This one's spoken for."

Gram straightened and gave George a sharp look. "I beg your pardon. I'm my own woman, thank you very much."

George's gaze roved over her in warm approval. "Yes, you are," he murmured.

Gram chuckled softly, and Kelsey decided she couldn't stand anymore.

"I need to get back to work. See you all later." She turned and headed toward the kitchen, but Luke caught up with her.

"You weren't kidding about George and your grandma. Those are some serious fireworks." He blew out a whistle. "See you Saturday." He tossed her a sexy, lopsided grin that made her wonder if she could feel fireworks again too.

Maybe on Saturday, she'd find out.

Chapter Seven
♀

IT WAS NEARLY six when Luke strolled up Main Street to pick up Kelsey. She was already standing on the sidewalk, waiting. He quickened his pace.

Kelsey smiled at him in greeting, raising her hand in a friendly wave. "Hey, Luke."

"Hey there, nice night, right?" The day had been uncharacteristically warm, and though it had cooled off, it was still very pleasant. He wore a long-sleeved T-shirt with a flannel button-down thrown over it. It was just right for this temperature, but after looking at Kelsey, he wished he'd taken a little more care with his appearance. Maybe worn his favorite field jacket.

Skinny jeans encased her sexy legs and terminated in dark brown suede ankle boots. She wore an olive-green jacket with a light patterned scarf, and her dark hair hung past her shoulders in long, glossy waves. She was stunning.

He tried not to stare, but it was hard. "You look great."

"Thanks. You do too. I like that shirt."

He glanced down at his favorite flannel and still wished he'd worn the jacket instead. "You're too kind. Most of my wardrobe makes me look like a lumberjack."

She laughed. "Goes with your perennial stubble."

He brushed his hand along his jaw, feeling the scratch of hair against his fingertips. "I hope that's a good thing."

"It's certainly not bad." She said this with a twinkle in her eye, and he had the distinct, wonderful feeling that she was flirting with him. "Ready?"

"Absolutely."

He pivoted so that she could walk up beside him, and they strolled to the corner. The Oktoberfest was held in the park, which was a mere two blocks away. They paused to look before they crossed the street. The Arch and Vine was on the opposite corner.

"Do you usually have Saturday nights off?" he asked.

"Most of the time. Sometimes I fill in for people, but generally speaking, it's one of my two days off from the pub. The other being Monday."

They moved past the pub. "So you don't have a weekend?"

She shook her head. "Not really. I get Mondays. No pub. No library."

"Except you said you usually work. Do you ever plan to cut back?"

She shrugged. "I don't know why I would."

He glanced up at the almost clear, darkening sky. "Maybe you'll fall madly in love and want to start a family or something crazy like that."

She slid him a probing look. "Is that what you want?"

He'd walked right into that one. And he actually didn't mind. "I don't know. I can honestly say I really haven't thought that far ahead. I figure those are things that happen…later."

She paused as they reached the next corner. "I'd agree with that sentiment. I'm quite content with my life as it is. I'm busy. I love my job. It's all good."

Across the street, the park was lit up and lined with

booths selling food, beer, and various arts and crafts. The party vibe was loud and joyous.

They crossed to the entry gate, where Luke paid the admission, which was actually a donation to charities benefiting the local area. "Where should we go first?"

They meandered into the central area, where tables were set up in clusters. A band was on stage at the other end of the park. Right now it was playing something that had all the kids up and dancing in a pint-sized mosh pit.

She glanced around. "I don't know. I guess I could go for a beer?"

"Beer it is." He reached to touch her lower back but wasn't sure if he should. Why not? This was a date. He'd told her so, and she hadn't balked. He let his hand graze the base of her spine as they moved toward the beer garden.

She slid him a quick look but didn't say anything. Nor did she step away.

At the beer garden, they flashed their IDs and the enforcement officer gave them wristbands, which they had to don immediately.

The beer was usually only from Archer, but last year, they'd invited another brewery to join them. This year, that brewery was back, plus two more. Brewers had clamored for the chance, but Rob Archer had invited small, up-and-coming breweries. He'd always gone out of his way to help others, and this was just another way he was doing that.

It was louder here in the tent, since the sound was contained. He leaned close to her and caught the scent of honeysuckle. "What's your poison?"

"I think I'd like to try the Brigand."

That was one of the new invitees. "I've heard good

So Right

things about them," he said. "Let's give it a go, shall we?"

They walked to the Brigand counter and ordered their pints. Along with the noise, it was warmer in here than outside. Once they had their beers, he asked if she wanted to go outside. At her nod, they moved through the crowd to the back door, which led into a contained outdoor area with tables. There was, however, nowhere to sit.

"Luke!"

He turned at the sound of his name and recognized Liam Archer standing over near the white picket fence that provided the enclosure. He was the oldest of the Archer sextuplets and ran the Archers' real estate interests. He was also a bit of a thrill seeker and had taken Luke and his brothers skydiving last summer.

Luke waved at him and leaned close to Kelsey once more. "Do you know Liam Archer?"

"Not well."

"Come on." He slipped his hand against her lower back again, this time touching her a little more firmly.

They walked to Liam and his wife, Aubrey, who clutched a glass of water and, frankly, looked a bit pale.

"Hey, Aubrey, everything okay?" Luke asked.

Aubrey offered a wan smile. "Just peachy."

Liam put his arm around her and pulled her against him. "I think we're going to have to go. Mama-to-be here is suddenly feeling…well, not great." He pressed a kiss to her temple.

Luke hadn't known they were expecting. "Congratulations! Do you know Kelsey McDade?" He kept his hand against her back.

Kelsey nodded at Aubrey. "I think we've met."

Aubrey sipped her water. "Yes. You're the awesome

librarian, and you're putting together the Ribbon Ridge exhibit that I've heard so much about. I'd love to help in some way, if I can. I think my uncle has some photographs and other items he'd loan you. He and my aunt have been on an extended vacation the past several weeks, but they're due back shortly. I'll get in touch with you."

Kelsey grinned. "Thanks, I'd love that." She looked toward Liam. "How are you?"

"Good, thanks. My mom raves about your library. I need to stop in."

"You should. We're open every day but Mondays and Wednesdays."

Aubrey's pallor took on a greenish tinge. "Okay, babe, I need to go."

"Let's hit it." Liam slammed the rest of his beer and slid them an apologetic glance. "Sorry we have to bail. But here come Tori and Sean. See you guys."

Tori was another of the Archer sextuplets, and Sean was her British husband. She was a successful architect, while Sean operated a production company with Alaina Archer.

"Hey, Tori, Sean." Luke reached out and shook Sean's hand. He was a cool dude.

Tori smiled at them. "Hi, Kelsey, Luke. What're you drinking?"

Kelsey winced. "Don't shoot us, but it's Brigand."

Tori leaned forward and looked side to side before whispering, "We're drinking that too. Shhh. Don't tell my dad. Or Bex."

Hayden's wife, Bex, was the brewmaster at the pub located at the hotel the Archers owned in the hills above Ribbon Ridge. And of course Rob Archer had started Archer Brewing and still handcrafted new

So Right

recipes that were brewed at their ten-plus brewpubs.

"Wait, is that George?" Sean asked, pivoting toward the tent flap.

George and Ruby moved out of the tent. They were a handsome couple. George was tall and still very athletic, his gun-metal gray hair cropped close to his head in a not-quite-military cut. Ruby was small, almost petite, really, with short white hair styled immaculately so it swept back from her face.

"It is," Tori said. She turned to look at Kelsey. "And is that your grandmother? I met her at my folks' house the other morning. I stopped by during a run. She's a hoot."

"Yes, that's Gram," Kelsey said.

"Are they an item?" Tori asked, her eyes lighting. "That would be so great."

"I don't know what they are, but they seem to be having a good time."

Tori grinned. "That's all that matters. We all just adore George. There's nothing we'd like more than to see him find love." She put her arm around Sean and snuggled close against him.

Suddenly, Luke wanted to find love. Or at least companionship. For the first time, he missed what he'd had with Paige. Not that exactly, but the promise of something...special.

He thought about what he and Kelsey had talked about on the way over, how when he thought of long-term relationships and settling down, he always assumed that would come later. But when was later?

They chatted for a few more minutes, and then he and Kelsey decided to grab some food. They finished their ale before heading out of the beer garden.

On the way out, they ran into Brooke and Cam, who

were hand in hand. "Hey, bro!" Cam clapped Luke on the shoulder as Brooke and Kelsey exchanged a brief hug.

"We're headed for some of Kyle's killer fondue." Another of the Archer sextuplets, Kyle was a celebrity chef and ran the restaurant up at The Alex hotel.

Brooke looked over at Cam. "Oh, that sounds so good. Can the beer wait?"

"Whatever my love wants is my fondest desire." Cam took her hand and pressed a kiss to her palm.

"I think I might gag," Luke said.

Kelsey nudged him in the arm. "Don't say that. It's cute."

"He's my brother. There's a law that I have to give him crap. You have a brother, right?"

"Yes, but he's ten, so it's not remotely similar. Plus, I don't think the dynamic between brothers and sisters is quite the same as just brothers."

"Or just sisters," Brooke put in. "I have two of those, and I can attest to taunting them as much as these yokels do." She jabbed her thumb toward Luke and Cam.

They turned and headed toward the fondue booth. A space at a table opened up, so Brooke and Kelsey grabbed spots for them while Luke and Cam went to get the food.

Cam looked over at the ladies with their heads bent together. "You didn't tell me you were coming with Kelsey tonight." He speared Luke with an inquisitive stare.

Luke shrugged. "No big deal."

"Tell that to Mom. If she sees that you're on a date, she'll have Kelsey over for dinner faster than you can say chicken potpie."

Luke looked around. "Is she here?"

Cam stepped forward as the line moved. "Probably. She and Dad usually come on Saturday night."

"Well, do me a favor and keep your mouth shut."

"Is it a secret?" Cam asked.

Luke sent him an exasperated stare. "Obviously not, but as you pointed out, Mom will be all over this like ugly on a gorilla."

"Eh, it's not that bad. Brooke loves her."

"Good for Brooke." Luke didn't want to scare Kelsey off. Mom could be intense.

It was their turn at the counter, and they ordered fondue, sausage, and pretzels. They had to wait nearly ten minutes for the food and then carted it back to the table.

Kelsey looked up at Luke as he sat down next to her. "So we just got a text from Crystal. She's in California this weekend, but she set up an appointment with the archaeologist this Wednesday at eleven. Does that work for you guys?" She glanced over at Cam before returning her gaze to Luke.

"Works for me," Cam said.

Luke broke off a piece of pretzel. "Yep, I can do that. Do you know what the meeting will entail?"

Brooke answered. "Crystal said the archaeologist will do a walk on the property and a cursory search. Apparently, there are things she might be able to see without even digging."

Cam leaned his arm on the table. "Really? That's fascinating. I'm really looking forward to this. And I know Jamie is too. Crap, he might be gone that day. I think he's signed up for some accounting workshop or something."

"We could probably reschedule," Kelsey said.

Luke heard a hint of disappointment in her tone. "Nah, we can go ahead. I imagine the archaeologist will need to come back. Jamie will get a chance to nerd out."

"Hey, archaeology isn't nerdy," Brooke said. "Look at Indiana Jones." She sent a knowing glance at Kelsey, who nodded in agreement.

"Yeah, because all archaeologists look like that and have the opportunity to swashbuckle."

Kelsey shook her head at Luke. "That's not a verb. You're trying to use that as a verb."

"Why can't it be? To swashbuckle. I like it." He grinned at her, and she rolled her eyes.

"The point is," Brooke said sternly but with a smile, "archaeology isn't nerdy."

"I didn't mean that it was," Luke said, holding up his hands in mock defense. "I only meant that it's a subject about which Jamie is interested, or dare I even say excited. Maybe he'll go back to school and get a fourth—or would it be his fifth?—degree in that field."

"Hello!" Mom's singsong greeting made the hair on Luke's neck stand up. He swiveled his head around to see her quickly approaching the table with Dad. "How wonderful to run into my boys."

"Hi, Mom," Cam said.

Brooke jumped up and gave her a quick hug. "Do you want my seat?"

"No, no. We're on our way out." Her gaze was fixed on Kelsey.

Luke stood. "Mom, this is my friend Kelsey McDade. Kelsey, this is my mom, Angie. And my dad, Sam."

Mom shook Kelsey's hand and then Dad did the same. "Pleased to meet you," Dad said, "though I feel as though we've met before."

"I work at The Arch and Vine," Kelsey said.

Dad smiled. "That's it."

"Is that right?" Mom asked. "So you're a waitress?"

"And a librarian," Luke answered. "She runs the new library in town."

Mom cocked her head to the side. "I was in there last week, and I don't think I saw you."

Kelsey clasped her hands on the edge of the table in front of her. "If you came in on a Thursday or Friday, you probably met Marci. She's my assistant. I was likely upstairs working on the Ribbon Ridge exhibit."

Mom laughed the kind of laugh that came from anxiety or discomfort. "Oh yes, of course. How silly of me. Brooke's told me all about that. I didn't realize you were one of the women she mentioned was working with her." She waved her hand. "My bad. It's lovely to meet you finally. And you're here with Luke?" Mom smiled expectantly as she glanced from Kelsey to Luke and back to Kelsey again.

"Uh, yes." Kelsey flicked a look toward him. It wasn't panic. No, nothing so dramatic, but there was a shadow of apprehension there.

Time to come to the rescue. "So you and Dad are headed home? Any booths we need to see?"

"Oh yes, make sure you head toward the play structure," Mom said. "There's a young man over there displaying his art, and it's just fantastic."

Luke sat back down, hoping they'd go on their way. He sent Dad a pleading look. "Thanks for the tip. We'll check it out."

Dad brushed his hand along Mom's back. "Come on, dear. I'm beat after trimming the shrubs today." He clapped Cam on the shoulder, since he was closer. "See you boys later. Good night, Brooke—and Kelsey." He smiled warmly as he escorted Mom away.

"So who wants to go see art?" Brooke had sat back down but now got up again.

"Me," Cam said, picking up their trash. He looked across the table at Luke and Kelsey. "You coming?"

Luke turned toward his date, and she nodded as she said, "Sure."

After disposing of their trash, they made their way to the arts and crafts on display and for sale. The watercolorist was quite good. He'd done a rendering of a vineyard, which Luke couldn't seem to tear his eyes from.

Kelsey came to stand beside him. "You like that a lot." She was close enough that he could smell her intoxicating honeysuckle scent.

"I do."

"It's gorgeous."

He turned and whispered, "Not as pretty as you."

"Now you're just being corny."

"Nope. I'm being honest." He took her hand and squeezed it before turning to continue to the next booth.

When she didn't withdraw her hand, his pulse quickened. The next booth was handmade jewelry— earrings and bracelets, mostly.

Kelsey picked up a silver bracelet from the display. A book charm dangled from the clasp. "Cute," she murmured.

"You like that?"

She nodded. "I'm a sucker for silver. And books." She smiled at the vendor as she set it back down.

They caught up with Brooke and Cam and had a good time touring the booths until Cam realized they'd never gone to the beer garden. Kelsey didn't really want to go back, and Luke didn't either. Instead, they made their way to the music area where the headlining act had just taken the stage. They were playing something in between a fast and slow song, and Luke asked Kelsey to dance.

"Seriously? I don't remember the last time I danced."

"Me neither." He shrugged, smiling at her. "Sounds fun, though, right? And this is a good song."

"I can't argue with you there, but don't laugh at me, okay?"

"Only if you promise not to laugh at me."

He led her to the dance floor, which was basically an open area of grass currently populated by maybe a dozen people. They did their best to dance and twirl to the song, laughing as they collided more than once as they each tried to figure out what to do.

The song ended, and, still giggling, they traipsed back toward the periphery.

She looked up at him. "I've had a great time, but I've got a double shift tomorrow with the library and the pub."

"But Cinderella, it's nowhere near midnight."

She pointed her toe. "And I'm not wearing glass slippers. Sorry to burst your fantasy."

Yes, she was a fantasy, he realized. A living, breathing dream of what he wanted right now.

"Come on, I'll walk you home." He twined his fingers through hers, and they made their way out of the park.

She cast a sidelong glance his way. "You live near here, right?"

"Go a block west and then up three more blocks. Tiny rental. Okay, maybe not tiny, and it's about to get bigger. Did I tell you that Jamie's moving out?"

She looked at him askance as they crossed the street. "No, you didn't. Is that a good thing?"

"Yes. I prefer to live alone."

She mock-gasped and widened her eyes. "Me too."

He grinned at her, enjoying her company so much. "Shocker."

She laughed softly, the sound cascading over him like a cozy blanket. "Where's he moving to?"

"Brooke's old loft. He just managed to snag it right after she gave notice."

"Damn."

Luke stopped on the sidewalk. "What's wrong?"

"She told me that she was moving and asked if I was interested in taking her loft. Stupidly, I said no."

She was the person Cam had mentioned. That sucked. She looked so disappointed.

Maybe he could ask Jamie not to take it. Which, of course, meant that Luke would still have a roommate.

She narrowed her eyes at him. "Don't you dare talk to Jamie. It's his fair and square. Anyway, my initial response was to pass, and sometimes your gut just knows what to do. I'm going to trust that."

"Are you sure?"

She nodded vigorously. "Absolutely. Jamie deserves it—and you deserve to have your own place. I can see how much it means to you."

She was quite simply the best woman he'd ever met. "Can I kiss you?"

She stared at him, her lips parting slightly. He heard the small but distinctive intake of her breath.

He leaned forward.

She jerked away but didn't let go of his hand. "Ask me again when we get to my place. Sorry, I need to…process."

He forced himself to take a deep breath. His pulse was working overtime, and points south of his waistband were getting ahead of themselves.

"So your parents seem nice."

Now he knew she was the best woman. His mother ought to have scared her off. "My mom didn't make you cringe with the waitress comment? You have a freaking master's degree, for crying out loud."

She laughed. "I'm used to that. You should see how some customers treat waitstaff. It's disgusting."

He hated that she had to put up with that. They turned the corner and headed back toward The Arch and Vine. "But she's my mother."

"And I'm sure she's lovely. I told you a bit about my mother, right? She would've asked how many dates we'd gone on and whether we planned to go out again. And our answers would've just spurred more questions. It's always an interrogation with her."

"Yikes, sorry."

They crossed the street again, and he was torn between walking faster to see if he'd get to kiss her and slowing to a crawl because he didn't want the evening to end. Although, if he kissed her and things progressed…maybe the evening wouldn't end at all.

Whoa there, pal. Settle.

They got to her door, and she turned toward him. "And here we are." She looked up at him, and her eyes were pale and gorgeous in the lamplight.

"About that kiss…"

She slid her hands up his shirtfront and clasped the sides of his jaw. Coming up on her toes, she pressed her lips against his. Her touch raced through him like electricity—hot and blinding. He grasped her waist and pulled her close until her hips grazed his.

She pulled her lips from his but didn't retreat. Her eyes opened, and the vulnerability in their depths stole his breath. "I haven't done that in years. I don't…" She shook her head.

He lifted his hands and cupped her face. "Thank you." He kissed her again, softly moving his mouth over hers, wanting more but afraid to take anything she didn't want to offer.

Her hands slipped down his neck and clutched at his collar. She pulled him closer and twined her hands around his nape. Then she angled her head and opened her mouth. That was the invitation he'd been waiting for. The fantasy he'd been dreaming of.

He thrust his fingers into the sleek softness of her hair as her tongue danced against his. Sensations exploded—her scent filling his nostrils, the sound of his heartbeat thundering in his ears, the spark of heat igniting inside him, the feel of her body pressed along his.

He kissed her like he hadn't been kissed in years. And he hadn't—not like this. It was like unwrapping a present he hadn't asked for. A gift he hadn't known he wanted, and yet suddenly didn't think he could live without.

She arched against him. Desire pulsed through his veins, heightening his arousal. He wanted to ask if he could take her upstairs when someone wolf-whistled from across the street.

She pulled away, bringing her hand to her mouth as she presented her back to the street. Her cheeks were flushed, her gaze fixed on her door.

"Can I walk you up?" His voice was deeper than normal. More primal.

"No." She swallowed as she turned to face him, her eyes glazed and maybe a bit…wild. "I had a great time tonight. Truly. I…I like kissing you. I'm attracted to you. But—" She turned back toward the building and inhaled slowly before exhaling just as slowly. She did this two more times, as if it were some sort of breathing exercise.

Then she pivoted back again, looking slightly calmer—more serene—than she had a moment before. "I don't think I can do this. I'm not ready."

"Do what?" He wanted to be clear. "I have all the patience in the world."

She shook her head. "It's more than…*that*. It's everything. I'm not ready for a relationship."

"Then we'll be friends for now. Or forever. If that's what you want. I'm here to stay, Kelsey."

"What if I don't want you to?" The question was low and stark, and it sliced into him like the sharpest, most well-aimed knife.

He sensed she needed a very specific answer to that. An answer that would give her the freedom she needed. That she deserved. He could only imagine the hell she'd gone through, and damn it, he wanted to understand. But now wasn't the time to ask for that—and it might never come. "Then I'll go."

She stared at him another moment, blinking, before turning to unlock the door and fleeing upstairs. He stood there and stared at the closed door.

And then he did what he said he'd do—he left.

Chapter Eight

KELSEY PARKED IN the lot at West Arch Estate and shut off the car just before eleven on Wednesday. She sat there for a moment and took a deep breath. She hadn't seen Luke since last Saturday night when she'd kissed him. They'd texted some, mostly about today's meeting with the archaeologist, but she'd held back a little. She couldn't help it.

Crystal pulled into the spot next to her and waved.

Kelsey stepped out of the car and pocketed her keys. The day was cool, with thick clouds overhead. The forecast called for rain, but hopefully it would hold off until they were finished. Just in case, she'd worn her rain boots.

Crystal had done the same. As she came around her car to meet Kelsey, she pointed at their boots. "Same pair!"

Kelsey wiggled her toes. "I love these." Living in the Pacific Northwest her whole life, she knew the value of good rain boots.

"Me too. I didn't realize how important and fabulous rain boots could be until I started spending more time here," Crystal said.

They walked toward the winery. "Is it hard to travel so much?" Kelsey asked.

Crystal lifted a shoulder. "I'm used to it. Mostly it's here to LA, so it's not terrible. Flying back and forth to North Carolina gets old, so I only go a few times a year.

And usually for Thanksgiving and Christmas. My family gives me such a hard time if I miss the holidays. I haven't told them yet, but I'm actually thinking of staying here for Christmas this year." She winced. "Maybe. I have to decide if I'm up for the battle."

Kelsey hadn't spent the holidays with her family in years. Noah wouldn't have let her even if she'd wanted to. And she'd spent the last two Christmases working. "That's a bummer."

As Crystal reached for the door, the sound of a car pulling into the lot behind them made them turn. It was a blue Prius. Kelsey didn't recognize the driver.

Crystal turned from the door. "Must be the archaeologist."

"Must be," Kelsey agreed.

The woman stepped out of the car and waved at them. "Hi, I'm Dana Boyd."

Kelsey and Crystal went to shake her hand and introduced themselves.

"Thanks so much for coming out here today," Crystal said. "Can we help you with anything?"

Dana had shoulder-length brown hair and wore a stylish khaki cap with a narrow brim and a pair of glasses with a purple rim. Kelsey would say she was in her late thirties, but wasn't great at guessing ages. Dana smiled as she reached into the backseat. "Nope, I'll just get my bag."

"Love your hat," Kelsey said. "Can I ask where you got it?"

Dana frowned briefly, then pulled it off. "Had to remember which one I grabbed. I'm a total hat whore."

Kelsey grinned. "Me too."

"REI, I think," Dana said, looking inside the hat. She found the tag. "Yep. But it was a few years ago. I like your hat too."

Kelsey's was a dark gray cap with a bit of a newsboy flair to it.

Crystal pivoted back toward the winery. "Come on, we'll meet everyone else inside."

"Sounds good." Dana locked her car, and they moved into the building. Brooke, Cam, and Luke were waiting in the large main room, which was nearly finished—good thing since their wine club dinner was this weekend.

Crystal took care of introducing everyone. They had a good-sized group but were still missing some folks. Alaina's daughter was under the weather today, so Alaina hadn't been able to make it. Hayden was too busy, and Jamie had something else going on.

Kelsey had tried not to look at Luke as soon as she'd come inside, but couldn't keep her gaze from wandering in his direction. He was looking at her too. She gave him a small smile, but he didn't return it. His eyes were dark, sort of intense. She remembered his lips on hers and shivered.

Dana looked around at all of them. "Shall we head up to the alleged site of the homestead?"

"Yes, this way," Cam said, leading them toward the staircase and the hall beyond that, which led to an exterior door.

Once they were outside, Dana opened her bag and withdrew a map, which she unfolded and perused. "Let me just get my bearings." She looked out over the vineyard and then back to the map. Then she folded it back up. "Okay, so we're heading up there?" She pointed to the top of the ridge.

"That's what we thought," Crystal said.

Luke took the lead. "We'll go through the vineyard."

Dana walked toward the front with Luke, Cam, and Crystal, while Kelsey hung back with Brooke.

"How'd things go the other night?" Brooke asked in a near whisper.

Kelsey kept her voice low. "Fine."

Brooke cast her a skeptical look. "Uh-oh. Not good? Or great?"

It had actually been pretty awesome. Right up until she'd told him she couldn't see him. "It *was* good." She gauged how much to reveal. Being with Noah had trained her to keep things to herself. She should open up. But damn, it was hard. "Things ended on a bit of an awkward note."

"Oh no! What happened? Kiss gone bad?"

Kelsey laughed, which drew the folks in front to turn and look. Everyone but Luke, who just kept walking. Sobering, Kelsey looked down at the dirt beneath her boots as they hiked up between the vines. "No, actually. The kiss…es were fabulous."

Brooke grinned. "'Kisses'? Doesn't sound awkward."

"Well, that part came after. When I basically fled the scene. It's just been a long time since I've done that. I'm so out of practice." If only it were that simple.

"Cut yourself some slack. There is absolutely no rush—trust me, I know." She'd been divorced, and it had taken a while for her to be ready to date. Even when she'd met Cam, she'd been reluctant, so yeah, she definitely understood that part. "And everything I know about Luke tells me he'll be patient. Is he being a dick?" She lowered her voice to ask that last question.

Kelsey's gaze latched onto his back. He wore a slouchy hooded sweatshirt and beat-up jeans that rode his hips perfectly. She recalled the feel of his body against hers, and warmth pulsed through her. "No, he's not being a dick." He *was* being a little standoffish today.

Or was he? It wasn't as if she'd made a point of saying hello to him. Nor had she tried to walk with him. Out of practice maybe didn't fully describe how bad she was at this.

"Things will even out," Brooke said. "It takes time to work through that new-and-awkward phase."

They crested the hill, and Dana stopped. She set her bag down and surveyed the area. Then she turned and addressed everyone. "So this looks quite a bit different than it did almost a hundred and fifty years ago when they decided to build a house up here. You might ask why they did that. Or maybe you didn't—that's what we archaeologists wonder." She smiled. "It's removed from the town, which is odd, but you can definitely see it from here." She gestured down to where Ribbon Ridge lay below.

"Why would they build up here?" Cam asked.

"Like I said, it looked different. The map shows a flatter area here as well as a spring." She turned and walked to where the flat land sloped down into a shallow ravine. "Down there. If we dig a little, we'll find water. This is where it's marked on the map."

Luke followed her and looked down into the ditch. "Wow, can I use that for irrigation?"

Dana shrugged. "Probably." She pivoted and looked back over the flat area, where everyone was still standing. "Can I get you all to scoot that way?" She held her arm straight out and pushed it to her right.

They moved over, and Dana tipped her head to the side as she stared at the ground.

Luke, still beside her, put his hands on his hips. "What do you see?"

She walked forward and gestured in front of her. "See how the grass is just a bit different here? You can almost see a line. She marched along the line, which Kelsey could barely make out, then turned sharply. After several steps, she turned again, then repeated the process. "That's the house."

Crystal's jaw dropped, and she shook her head. "Wait, that's it? You look at the ground, and you can see this?"

Dana grinned. "I've been doing this a long time. That's just my supposition. Let's see if I'm right." She went back to her bag and fished out a small shovel with a flat edge. Going back to one of the corners, she crouched down and scraped along the surface, moving grass and dirt. "This all started when you found a brick, is that right?"

Brooke nodded. "Yes, it was part of a newer house that was built on the property. It says 1879 and BNR, and our research led us to find Bird's Nest Ranch."

"I'd say the brick was from the foundation of this house." She held up a small, dark chunk. It looked like rock, not brick. Standing, she held it in her palm. "This is brick. If we excavate, we'll find a lot more of it."

Everyone crowded around her and peered down at her hand.

"Wow, how can you tell that's brick?" Crystal asked. "It's black."

Dana handed her the piece of brick. "That's the interesting part. It's scorched. I'd say this house burned down."

Just like when they'd met with the historian and learned that Dorinda had died, there was a collective intake of breath. Crystal, Brooke, and Kelsey exchanged looks, and Kelsey was sure they were thinking the same thing.

"Can you find out when the fire happened?" Kelsey asked.

"We can send the brick pieces out for testing. We should be able to get close."

Crystal handed the piece of brick to Kelsey. "That would be great. We'll definitely want to do that."

Dana nodded. "Can do. The next thing we need to determine is whether this is eligible for the national historical registry. I need to obtain concurrence from the state historic preservation office that this is a nonsignificant site. I don't think that'll be a problem."

Luke turned toward her. "What if it is? Is someone going to want to come out here and dig up my vineyard?"

"It's possible, but highly unlikely."

Luke frowned, looking rather disgruntled. "Keep us posted, please." He glanced around the group. "I need to take care of some things." He took off down the slope.

Kelsey's chest tightened as she watched him go. He seemed more than standoffish. She wanted to follow him but didn't.

They finished up with Dana, who said she'd come back tomorrow and collect samples for testing. Cam walked her back to the parking lot so that Brooke, Kelsey, and Crystal could talk about what they'd found.

Crystal voiced what they were all thinking. "Do you think she died in the fire?"

Brooke's eyes were sad. "I don't want to think so."

Kelsey didn't want to either. For some reason, she had the sense that Dorinda's story wasn't a happy one. "I guess we'll find out when Dana does the testing."

"What was up with Luke?" Crystal asked. "Is he

against this?"

"He's against having his vineyard messed up," Kelsey said. "And I get that. I think he's just annoyed with me."

Brooke stroked Kelsey's arm. "It can't be just that."

"I did tell him I couldn't have a relationship with him after we had an incredible date." Kelsey massaged her forehead. "So yeah, I think it can be just that."

Crystal came and stood on her other side. "Yikes, sorry. But I have to ask why you told him that. Just not feeling it?"

On the contrary. She'd been feeling all sorts of things, especially while they were kissing. She'd actually considered inviting him upstairs. But then she'd thought about what could happen after that. She'd thought about all she didn't know about him. It wasn't that she didn't trust him—she didn't trust herself. What if she didn't know how to choose a decent guy?

But Luke is a decent guy, her mind argued.

The sting of her shame and pain weighed on her soul. "Actually, I had a great time with him. I like him a lot. I'm just…not ready." They both looked at her, and she knew they wanted to ask why but also didn't want to push. "You guys are really good friends," she said, wiping at the sudden dampness that had leapt to her eyes.

Brooke's hand moved to Kelsey's upper back, and she rubbed little circles over her shoulder blades. "Oh, Kel, what's wrong?"

"You know I used to date a guy, right?"

"Yeah, but that's about it."

It was such a long and horrible story. Well, the beginning wasn't. The beginning had been a fairy tale. "His name was Noah, and he was my knight in shining

armor. He swept me up and saved me from the toxic
relationship between me and my mom. He was kind,
considerate, and I knew he would slay every dragon to
keep me safe. He was fierce and strong. And
opinionated. And domineering. And demanding." Her
voice got smaller with each word.

She took a deep breath and forced herself to
continue. "I was nineteen when he hit me for the first
time. We lived in a tiny off-campus apartment, and he
was upset because I was late coming home from a
study group. He cried and begged me to forgive him.
Of course I did. And it didn't happen again for over a
year. It's just like what you read about—this horrific
cycle of escalating abuse. I knew better. I just didn't
know how to make it stop. He loved me, and I loved
him. Even after he broke the bottle over my head,
requiring eleven stitches, and cracked my ribs, I didn't
want to leave. But I did. I cried when I made the report
to the police, because I knew his life would be ruined."
It had taken months and months of therapy for her to
accept that he'd ruined his life long before she'd made
that call. And if she hadn't, he would've ruined hers
too.

Neither Crystal nor Brooke said a word as they
crowded in against her and put their arms around her
in a tight hug.

Kelsey's eyes were surprisingly dry as she took in
their comfort and warmth. After a long minute, they
pulled apart, and Kelsey forced a weak smile. "Now
you know why I'm a broken mess."

Brooke dashed her hand over her eyes. "Sorry. I had
no idea. I feel so bad that I didn't know."

Kelsey touched her arm. "Don't, please. I didn't want
anyone to know. No one here knows. I think my boss

at The Arch and Vine might've suspected something with the weird injuries I had sometimes, but Noah was really good at hitting me where it wouldn't show. The times he fucked up were when he was really pissed—out of control."

Crystal's eyes hardened. "I want to kick this guy's ass so bad."

Kelsey cracked a smile. If anyone could, she thought Crystal had a good shot. She was an expert kickboxer and had a black belt in some sort of martial art. "You can't. He's in prison."

She frowned in legitimate disappointment. "Damn it. But I'm glad—for you."

Brooke shook her head. "I can't believe everything you've been through. And this was just a couple of years ago?"

"Yeah, really just a few months after we moved to the area. I think being here where no one knew me gave me the courage to do what I had to. I could sort of start over as a new person. Someone who wasn't a victim." It had been a good theory, but as she'd learned in therapy, shedding the victim mentality was hard.

"I get it," Brooke said. "My situation is different, but I felt so worthless after my divorce and after finding out I couldn't have children. I didn't think it was even possible for me to find love again. I understand why you'd want to take things slow with Luke."

Crystal nodded. "For sure. Do you have a therapist?"

"I do. I don't see her as much as I used to, but maybe I should make an appointment." Duh, Kelsey would do that as soon as she left. She'd love to figure out a way to see Luke without being petrified.

Hmm, one thing would be to just not be petrified. He was Luke—warm, funny, caring Luke. He wasn't

Noah. They were absolutely nothing alike. When she'd met Noah, sparks had flown immediately. With Luke, things were a much slower burn. They'd been acquaintances, then friends. And now, maybe, they could be more.

"Thanks, girls." She hugged them both, and they gave her a long squeeze.

"We're here for you," Brooke said.

Crystal squeezed her hand. "*Anytime.*"

They headed back toward the winery, and Kelsey felt lighter than she had in ages.

LUKE HADN'T REALLY had something pressing to do. He'd just wanted to get away from Kelsey. Being around her was torture. All he could think about was talking with her, laughing, touching, kissing. He'd retreated to the winery and now felt stupid. He'd have to learn to accept that she wasn't his girlfriend and likely never would be. It wasn't as if this were a breakup.

Why did it feel like one, then?

Cam came in from the parking lot. "Hey, were you pissed up there? With the archaeologist?"

Pissed was maybe extreme. "I'm not enthusiastic about someone tearing up my vineyard."

"Me neither. I'm sure it won't come to that." Cam eyed Luke and seemed to weigh whether he should say more. "Anything else?"

"Just spit it out." Like Luke couldn't figure out what he wanted to say.

"You and Kelsey seemed frosty. Did things not turn

out well the other night? You haven't said a word, and you're working the same relentless schedule."

That was true. He hadn't even taken the hike he'd planned on Monday. The hike where he'd wanted to take Kelsey to show her his Eagle Scout bridge.

No way was he going to say anything to Cam. Kelsey's issues were hers, and he wouldn't share them even to explain the dark cloud over his head. "Things turned out fine."

"You're a crappy liar, but whatever. I'm sorry. I like Kelsey a lot. You guys are cute together."

Were. They *were* cute together.

"I'm headed outside for a bit." Luke went downstairs and made his way out through the bottling room.

As he started up the slope, he caught sight of Kelsey. And she was coming straight for him.

Surprised, he kept walking and met her partway up the hill. They stood there for a moment just looking at each other. She wore one of her hats—a cute gray cap with a button decoration on the side. Her hair was loose beneath it, falling past her shoulders. The other night, he'd been lucky enough to touch it, and he'd reveled in its silky softness. Thinking that he would never touch it again was depressing.

She spoke first. "How are you?"

"Good."

She crossed her arms over her chest and cocked her hip. "I think you're lying. You seemed annoyed earlier."

"I'm concerned about the vineyard being dug up."

"Yeah, me too, but I think it'll be okay. You heard what Dana said. It's not historically significant." She narrowed her eyes slightly. "I don't think that's all, though. I think things are awkward now. Between us."

It sounded terrible when she said it out loud. He was

an adult. He could take rejection. "I'm sorry. I was disappointed." Except the emotion wasn't past tense, and he didn't know when it would be.

"I know. Me too. Which is stupid. If I'm disappointed, I could just change my mind, right?" She dropped her hands to her sides and stepped toward him. She was uphill, so he had to look up at her. "I never thought I'd want to date anyone again. After... I saw a therapist for a long time, and she said I might never be ready for a relationship again, but that it was up to me to try. If that's what I wanted." She sucked in a breath. "And... I do."

She wanted a relationship? With him? He didn't want to guess. He took a step so that his eyes were on level with her chin. "Are you saying you want me?"

She edged forward, coming down so that they were eye to eye. "I am saying that. I just want to be honest with you. I'm a mess. I don't know how this is going to work, but I'm willing to try. You said you have a lot of patience, and I hope that's true."

Joy unspooled inside him, and he couldn't contain a smile. He also couldn't keep from touching her. He slid his hands around her waist and pulled her against him.

"Yep, I happen to have scads of patience. A lifetime supply, in fact. I also have very good brakes. We'll go as slow as you want. And if you need to stop—at any time for any reason—we can do that too." He looked into her eyes, inspired by her courage. "You're an extraordinary woman, Kelsey. I don't fully comprehend what you've gone through, but I hope you'll tell me at some point." He reached up and traced his hand along her hairline, inadvertently touching her scar. He flinched and drew his hand away. "Sorry, I didn't mean to do that."

So Right

She gently shook her head. "It's okay. I don't want Noah to come between us. I won't let him. Maybe you could even make me forget he ever existed." Her blue eyes glinted with provocation.

He hardened in response. "I accept that challenge." He buried his hand in her hair and drew her against him as his mouth descended on hers.

Their kiss the other night had been soft, exploratory. This was hotter. Deeper. They knew the territory—at least a little—which meant they could traverse it fullbore. Like a familiar trail.

Only, the sensations cresting over him weren't familiar. They were new and exciting, and he couldn't get enough. He opened his mouth against hers, and their tongues collided. Her hands crept up his back and tugged at his shirt, and she pressed into him, their bodies touching from lips to chests to hips.

A raindrop hit his hand, but he ignored it in favor of losing himself in her embrace. She found the nape of his neck and tugged at the hair coming out from the bottom of his hat. He wanted to toss the damn thing off along with the rest of his clothing so she could run her hands all over him.

Her fingers dug into his neck as the kiss deepened. He clutched at her waist, pulling her against his groin. She moaned into his mouth, and it was the most erotic fucking thing he'd ever heard. If it were not broad daylight in the middle of his vineyard and raining, he'd drag her down to the ground right now.

Rain?

He was suddenly aware that it *was* raining, and they were about to get quite wet. He broke the kiss, gasping, and took her hand. "Come on!"

She glanced up at the sky and was rewarded with a

fat raindrop on her nose. He tipped his head and licked it off. She gave him a sultry stare as he pulled her toward the winery.

They ran for cover as the rain came down harder, dampening their clothes. Their laughter filled the air as they reached the underside of the patio above. There was only about four feet of covered space running along the edge of the building, but it was enough. He pulled her back into his arms and kissed her again, tasting heat and rain and desire.

Pivoting, she put her back against the building and pulled him between her legs. He was hard and eager, his cock finding that sweet spot as she rotated her hips against him.

She moaned into his mouth again, and he cupped her face, pinning her so he could taste his fill. She clasped his hips and held him as her head angled, and her tongue slid against his.

He felt a vibration and stupidly thought of a sex toy. She tugged her lips from his. "My phone." She kissed him again, quick and hard. "I would ignore it, but I had to find someone to work for me today, and she said she might have to pick her kid up from school because he had a cold."

He licked along her lips and pulsed his hips against hers. "Uh-huh."

She pulled the phone from her back pocket and held it up.

He pushed her hair to the side to access the creamy softness of her neck. Kissing her flesh, he said, "I hope this means you'll come to the wine dinner with me on Saturday. I can't wait to see you in a sexy dress and take you up to my office—"

She stopped moving, and he could've sworn her

body temperature took a nosedive.

She pushed at him, her eyes glued to her phone until she raised them, and he saw the stark fear in their ice-blue depths.

"My ex just got out of prison."

Chapter Nine
☙❧

KELSEY'S HAND SHOOK as she looked at the blaring text on her phone. She'd signed up for a text alert to be notified when Noah was released from prison. She hadn't thought it would be this early.

"He only served twenty months. It was supposed to be thirty-six. I knew it would probably be less, but I didn't think it would be that much." Her phone blurred, and she swayed.

Luke's arms caught her, and he held her by the waist. "I've got you."

His voice was cool and calming. She squeezed her eyes shut for a moment.

Noah was free.

Would he try to contact her? He wasn't supposed to, but that didn't mean he wouldn't try. He'd never been able to quash his impulses. She doubted twenty months in prison would've changed him. She hoped so—for his sake—but she never wanted to see him again.

She felt Luke's hands on her face, his lips against her temple. She opened her eyes. And his dark gaze was full of warmth and caring. She relaxed a bit.

"Nothing's changed here," he said. "I still care for you. I want to be here for you—however you need. *Whatever* you need."

She leaned into him, and his arms came around her, holding her tight. "Thank you. I can't really process this right now." She inhaled, and his fresh, outdoorsy scent filled her senses.

He ran his hands over her back in long, soothing strokes. Her pulse slowed, and she closed her eyes again, savoring this moment. Then she stepped back. "I need to go. I'm so sorry to drag you down with my problems. I won't blame you if you want to run far away."

He clasped her hand and squeezed her fingers. "I won't. And don't trivialize this. It's a big deal, and I get that."

God, he was amazing. She leaned forward and kissed his cheek. "I'll talk to you soon."

He nodded, and she made her way up to the winery, keeping close to the building to stay under the cover. A few minutes later, she was ensconced in her car and on her way back to town.

The text had included a phone number to call if she had questions. She put her headset on and dialed the number. She wanted to know when he'd been released and whether she should expect him. Fear carved an ache in her belly, a deep, painful throb that made her want to curl into a ball.

A woman answered the phone and transferred Kelsey to someone who could help her. She was afraid she'd be stuck leaving a message and then agonizing until she received a call back. However, luck smiled on her, and a live body picked up the phone.

The clerk was very helpful. She explained that Noah wasn't allowed to contact her and that she should notify the court if he did. His official release would happen tomorrow, and he was apparently moving back to Washington immediately where he'd be assigned to a local parole officer. They were allowing him to go back to Kennewick because his family was there, and they'd offer the best support to help with his reentry to society.

By the time she hung up the phone, Kelsey felt slightly better, but there was still a gnawing ache inside her, knowing he was out there terrified her.

Forcing herself to push through the anguish, she parked in her rented spot and hurried straight to the Knitty Gritty, where Gram was working today. She still hadn't mastered knitting, but she was trying. She said that if she spent less time with George, she'd figure it out. Then she'd laughed. Kelsey smiled, grateful for that happy thought, and tried to think of another.

Damn, it was hard. She felt cold and heavy and completely on edge, as if the slightest thing would send her into a panic attack. She'd had a couple of those after Noah had been arrested. She'd even called his mother to apologize. Wow, had that been a colossal mistake.

She began to shake again.

Don't think about that! Happy thoughts. The library. Gram. Luke.

And meditation.

She took in her deep, three-second breath, counted to three, and exhaled slowly for three more seconds. By the time she reached the store, she felt marginally better. At least she'd stopped shaking.

Gram sat behind the counter, her brow furrowed and her fingers clacking two needles together. She glanced up as the door swung closed, setting off the bell. "Kelsey, I'm so glad you came to rescue me from this infernal task." She threw the needles down onto the counter and stood.

Kelsey looked around. Thankfully, the store was empty. "Gram." Her voice sounded small and hurt, like

So Right

when she'd fallen out of the walnut tree and sprained her wrist in Gram's backyard when she was six.

Gram's eyes widened, and she came around the counter. "You look terrified. What's wrong?"

"Noah got out of prison."

Gram pulled her into a massive hug, the kind that only grandmothers could give. The familiar warmth and scent cloaked Kelsey in a protective cocoon, and she thought if she could just stay here, she'd be fine.

But of course, she couldn't.

After what felt like several minutes, during which Gram patted her back and murmured words of comfort, Kelsey pulled away. "He's getting out tomorrow and moving back to Kennewick."

"He can do that?" Gram asked.

"Apparently. It's better than having him here."

Gram looked at her with concern, her brow creasing. "Definitely. Do you think he'll try to contact you?"

"He's not supposed to."

"You should get a restraining order. Or does that happen automatically?"

Kelsey wasn't sure. "I'll call an attorney." She could go over to Aubrey Archer's office in person. It was just down the street. Did Aubrey even handle that kind of thing? It didn't hurt to ask.

Gram took her hands and frowned. "Sweetheart, you're ice-cold. Come sit down, and I'll make you some tea." She ushered Kelsey to the stool behind the counter and went in the back.

Kelsey stared at the window but didn't really see anything. Her mind was a tumult of fear and anxiety. She'd worked so hard to regain a normal life, and she felt as though the world had been pulled out from under her.

The bell on the door jingled, and she jumped, practically tumbling from the stool. She jerked her head toward the entrance, half expecting to see Noah.

He doesn't get out until tomorrow. And even then, he won't come after you. He never touched you in public. He wouldn't start now.

The pep talk she gave herself did nothing to ease her stress. Her gaze followed the customer, a middle-aged woman who'd smiled in her direction before moving to the racks of yarn along the back wall.

Gram emerged from the back, cradling a steaming mug. "Here, it's chamomile with some honey. You'll feel better."

Kelsey tried to summon a smile but couldn't. She took the cup and inhaled the sweet, soothing scent.

She lifted her gaze to Gram's. "I love you."

Gram kissed her forehead. "I love you too, sweetheart."

The customer came to the counter, and Kelsey sipped her tea while Gram rang up her order. Soon they were alone in the shop once more.

"What are you going to do now?" Gram asked. "Do you want me to come stay with you tonight? Or maybe you want to come stay with me? The apartment has a pull-out couch."

Shit. Kelsey hadn't even thought that far ahead. Did she want to be alone? Not particularly. But he was still in prison for one more night at least. Even so, she just might not want to be alone. "I don't know. I think I'll be okay tonight."

Gram didn't look convinced, but she didn't say anything more about it. "Do you mind if I tell George about this? He was in the military, after all. I'm sure he'd be happy to kick Noah's ass if he ever comes near here."

Kelsey latched on to the new, much happier topic. "Are you and George serious? You just met him."

"True, but remember, your grandpa proposed to me after only three weeks, and we were married almost forty-five years." Her lips curved up, and a sparkle gleamed in her eye. "Sometimes it doesn't take long."

Like with Noah. Kelsey had fallen for him hard and fast. No, she wasn't going to trust that sort of timing ever again. But Gram was right in that it had worked out well for her. "So you like him a lot?"

Gram nodded. "I do. It's strange because I was confident I'd never have feelings for another man. I loved your grandfather so very much." She glanced away.

Kelsey touched her soft, wrinkled hand. "He'd want you to be happy. And for what it's worth, I think he'd like George." She'd thought that when she'd met him that first day she'd walked into The Arch and Vine. His jovial sense of humor had instantly reminded her of Grandpa.

Gram turned her head back, smiling. "I think so too." She shook her head and exhaled. "I don't know where we're going. But we're having a great time right now. I have to admit I love his place. He's got a vineyard, you know, and a filbert orchard."

"I bet that reminds you of Grandpa too." He'd raised trees, which he sold to wholesalers and nurseries.

"It does. And I think I could talk George into a goat and some chickens." She chuckled.

Kelsey laughed with her. "Uh-oh, that *does* sound serious."

Her equilibrium seemed to settle, and a half hour later, she felt much better. Good enough to walk to

Aubrey's office and talk to her about the restraining order, which she was more than happy to file.

Telling Aubrey about Noah had been difficult at first, but then the words had poured out. By the time Kelsey had finished, a surprising sense of calm and strength had descended over her. She actually thought she'd be okay.

But then it got dark, and as she sat in her apartment—alone—she had second thoughts. And third.

Her phone pinged, and as she had in the shop earlier, she jumped and nearly tumbled off the couch. Apprehensively, she picked it up from the arm of the sofa and looked at the screen.

Luke: *How are you doing? Can I bring you dinner?*

She didn't hesitate to type a response: *Yes, please.*

Luke: *What kind of pizza do you like?*

She tapped out her answer: *Hawaiian, but whatever you want is fine.*

Luke: *Hawaiian it is. See you in a few.*

Five minutes later, he texted again: *What's your favorite beer? I'm bringing a growler.*

She smiled, flattered that he'd thought of that too. She sent her answer, and in less than thirty minutes, he texted her again from downstairs. She leapt up and ran down to let him in. "Wow, you're faster than a delivery guy."

He gave her an exaggerated bow while holding the pizza box out in front of him. "At your service, my lady."

"So gallant." She held the door while he bent to pick up the growler he'd set on the ground.

"I can carry that," she offered.

He shook his head. "The gallant gentleman carries

everything." He winked as he walked past her. She pulled the door closed, and it locked automatically. She double-checked it anyway.

"After you." He inclined his head toward the stairwell, and she went first.

He followed her into the apartment, and she prepared for his reaction. "Now you can see why I've never invited you up. It's not exactly Pottery Barn in here."

He stood in the middle of her living room and surveyed the tiny space. "Um, yeah. I was thinking the architecture would be pretty cool given the age of the building, and those built-ins there are very nice, but…can I ask why you live here?"

She took the growler from him and placed it on the tiny kitchen table shoved in the corner. "Have you tried looking for rental property in Ribbon Ridge?"

He followed her, setting the pizza on the table. "Actually, I have. Why do you think I've been living with my brother the past two years?" He opened the growler while she pulled two pint glasses from the shelf in the kitchen. "Forget I asked. I get it. But now I see why you wanted Brooke's loft, and I feel like crap for not insisting that you take it instead of Jamie." He took the glasses from her and filled them.

She grabbed a couple of plates and some napkins. "Do you need a knife and fork?"

He took one of her two chairs. "Hell, no. Pizza is meant to be messy and greasy and awesome. Especially when it's from Slice of Pi."

Kelsey set the plates and napkins on the table and sat down next to him. "I can't argue with that." Ribbon Ridge's pizza place was a hole in the wall, but it was the best pizza she'd ever had. And it was crafted by a retired math teacher, hence the clever name.

He lifted his glass in a toast. "To messy, delicious pizza."

She clacked her glass against his. "And sharing them with messy, delicious people. In case you were wondering, I'm messy and you're delicious."

He laughed before he took a drink. "That was a close one. A second later and I would've spewed Crossbow everywhere." He sipped his beer and set his glass down. "For the record, you're more than delicious. You're *scrumptious*."

She drank her beer, and heat flushed through her. She could blame the alcohol, but she knew it was the company.

He opened the box, and they dug into the pizza for a few minutes before he asked, "How'd the rest of your day go?"

"Okay. Gram talked me off the ledge, and Aubrey Archer is going to file a restraining order for me. She thinks it's a slam dunk."

"I should hope so." He wiped a napkin over his mouth and picked up another slice of pizza. "That's great. You seem like you're feeling better."

She could easily nod and continue on as though she were, but panic had started to set in just before he'd texted. "I was. But then it got dark. He's still in prison until tomorrow, but after that…I'm not sure I want to be alone. I think I'm going to go stay with Gram."

"At the Archers'?" He frowned. "That's a one-bedroom apartment. You'd be sleeping on the couch."

"I was doing that when Gram was here. It's better than being alone."

"I have a spare room, you know, and it just so happens that I have a futon."

She'd been about to take a bite of pizza but froze. Was he inviting her to stay with him?

"Uh, I'm not sure that's the best idea." Hadn't she just thought about how fast-moving relationships were a catastrophe? "I do appreciate the offer, though."

He set his pizza down and rested his arms on the table on either side of his plate. "Look, I'm not asking you to move in with me. Just stay with me until you feel comfortable. We'll be roommates. You'll have your own space. Granted, I only have one bathroom, but it's doable. Plus, we both work so much, we'll hardly ever see each other."

That sounded disappointing. "You make a good argument. I don't know..." She could think of a million reasons she shouldn't, and they all had to do with her crippling fear.

"Come on. My place is small, but it's a damn sight nicer than this joint."

She didn't doubt that. "But it would only be temporary."

"Whatever you want."

"I'll think about it." She did just that as they finished their dinner, and the conversation turned to the wine club dinner coming up that weekend.

She realized she never gave him an answer about that. "I'd love to go with you. If you still want me to."

He cringed. "Gee, I asked someone else in the hours since I invited you. Sorry."

Laughter erupted from her chest, and she was so glad he'd texted her about dinner. She thought about him leaving, about the darkness that would invade when she was alone and didn't think she could face it. "You're a jerk. Despite that, I'm going to come stay with you for a few days. On one condition."

He finished his beer. "Anything."

"No hanky-panky."

He laughed so hard, he snorted. "What year is this, 1953? Hanky-panky?"

She giggled. "What would you call it?"

He leaned back and huffed out a breath while he crossed his arms and adopted a pensive pose. "I don't know. Monkey business?"

She sputtered out a laugh. "Monkey business?" The laugh grew to a guffaw until near-hysteria set in as he joined her. She fought to take a breath and pushed out the word, "Chicanery?"

He howled even louder, slapping his hand on the table. "How about fooling around?"

Tears spilled from her eyes and her face began to hurt from laughing so hard. It was one of those conversations that probably wouldn't have been funny to anyone else, but in that moment, they were consumed by uncontainable hilarity. "We are firmly planted in 1953. There are apparently no words—none—to describe sexy times in twenty-first century speak."

"Sexy times works." He poured himself more beer and took a long drink. "God, I haven't laughed like that in a long time. Okay, so no sexy times. Does that include kissing? Because I'm kind of hoping I get to do that with you again soon."

"Wouldn't that be dangerous? I could see kissing leading to—let me borrow a word from 1953 again—*petting*, and petting leading to the aforementioned sexy times. In fact, I would argue that kissing *is* sexy times."

He pouted. "Damn, your argument is sound."

"So no sexy times while I'm staying with you."

"Wait, none at all? Or just none in the house?" He

looked at her with such hope in his gaze, and he was so gorgeous with his stubble and that square jaw and those dark, hot-as-coals eyes.

"Let me think about that." She stood up. "Do you mind cleaning up while I pack a few things?"

"Not at all."

"Thanks. Back in a few." She went to her bedroom and immediately wondered what in the hell she was doing. She should just go to Gram's.

Which was outside town, and she liked walking to both of her jobs. She'd be close enough at Luke's that she could run back here to grab something if she needed it.

She began packing stuff in her big duffel bag and thought about what to take. How long would she be there? A few days? Maybe they'd hate living together. Maybe this would put an end to her apprehension about starting a relationship because she simply wouldn't want to.

Somehow she didn't see that happening.

A bit of the anxiety she'd been battling all day stole over her, and she sank down on the edge of her bed. She told herself to breathe. Once the restraining order was in place, she'd feel better. Aubrey said she'd file it on Monday and that it would almost certainly be granted immediately. Then Kelsey could come back home and get back to business as usual.

Home?

This place had never felt *less* like a home, and she was suddenly thrilled to be going somewhere else, even if it was maybe not the best idea. It certainly wasn't the worst.

She jumped up and finished packing, then went to the bathroom to grab her toiletries. Ten minutes later, she hefted her duffel bag and met him in the living room. "Ready."

He swept up the growler, which was still almost half-full, from the table. "Excellent. Let me get your duffel." He took the bag from her and walked toward the door. "Can you grab the leftover pizza?" He nodded toward the table.

She plucked her jacket from the hook by the door and locked up as he started down the stairs.

"Where's your car?" he asked.

"I park it a few blocks away."

He opened the door to the sidewalk and stepped outside. "Okay, you really need to move. We're going to work on that too. Actually, if our roommate thing works out, you'll be all set."

She followed him and pulled the door shut. "You didn't like having a roommate."

"I didn't like having *Jamie* as a roommate. There's a big difference."

She chuckled. "Maybe you won't like me either. I thought we both valued alone time."

She started toward the corner, and he fell into step beside her.

He slid her a sexy glance. "Something tells me I won't mind spending time with you at all."

A spring leapt into her step as she walked toward the repair shop where she parked her car.

Fifteen minutes later, he'd directed her to his house, a little bungalow with a darling porch. "You didn't tell me your house was so cute! I've walked by here a hundred times, and it always catches my eye. Needs some flowers, though."

"You can fix that," he said. "Just pull into the driveway."

She parked next to his Jeep. "I can't plant flowers in October. Don't you know anything about plants?"

He grinned. "As it happens, I *do*. I mean in the spring."

As in five months from now? "Let's get through the next few days, shall we?"

"Ouch. Is that all I get? A few days?"

She loved this teasing, flirty thing they had going on. It was especially great for keeping her mind from turning down all sorts of dark paths. But she grew serious. "This is temporary. You get that, right?"

He saluted her. "Whatever you say, boss."

She rolled her eyes. "I'm being serious. Or at least I'm trying to be."

He gave her a level stare. "I know. And you *are* the boss—don't forget that." He opened the door and stepped out of the car.

Kelsey took a deep breath and hoped she wasn't about to make another colossal mistake.

Chapter Ten
ᘡ৵

RAIN BEAT AGAINST the window in Jamie's old bedroom, but it didn't wake Luke up. He'd spent a relatively restless night on the futon, both because it wasn't his comfortable queen-sized bed and because said bed currently housed his alluring new roommate.

Luke had insisted that she take his bed and he'd sleep on the futon. She'd fought him on it, but in the end, he'd said that her refusal meant they would both sleep on the futon. Together.

Sadly, she'd decided to use his bed.

He rolled over and looked at his phone. It was way early. He should try to sleep a little more. Ha. His morning wood was already raging, and thoughts of Kelsey across the hall weren't doing much to quell that.

There were ways to ease that discomfort—ways that wouldn't violate their no-sexy-times pact. Ways that didn't involve her. Sigh.

Realizing there was no point in trying to sleep, he got up and took a shower. After getting dressed, he went to the kitchen to make coffee.

He heard the telltale creak of his door as it opened and looked up to see Kelsey stretching as she emerged from the hallway. She wore long, plaid pajama pants and a dark red Henley. As she raised her arms, the shirt pulled against her chest, clearly showing that she was not wearing a bra. Her breasts curved deliciously beneath the fabric, their nipples drawing his hungry gaze.

"Morning," she rasped, and her just-woken voice did a number on his already taxed libido. What was the point in jacking off in the shower if you were going to get pent-up fifteen minutes later?

"Morning." He sounded as if he'd swallowed a bag of glass. "Coffee?"

"Sure, thanks. What time do you usually head to work?"

"Depends. I'll probably take off soon." Because if he didn't, he might have to take another shower.

He poured her a cup of coffee and set it on the island in the center of the kitchen. "Milk or sugar? I think Jamie might've left some vanilla creamer."

She padded into the kitchen. "That sounds great."

He opened the fridge to check the bottle. It also gave him something to do besides stare at the sexy mess of her dark hair tumbling over her shoulders. "Hmm. The date on it is today." He set the creamer next to the steaming mug.

"I'll risk it." She opened the bottle and poured a healthy dollop into her coffee. "Thanks." She smiled as she lifted the cup.

What the hell had he been thinking inviting her to stay here and then agreeing to no sexy business, not even kissing?

He abruptly spun about and found a travel mug for his coffee. After filling it, he turned. "Time for work. I'll, uh, see you later?"

She nodded. "I'll be late. I work at the library today and then a shift at The Arch and Vine until eleven thirty."

He felt a mixture of disappointment and relief. It meant they wouldn't spend time together, but it also meant he wouldn't be tortured. In fact, he'd try to get to sleep before she even came home.

"The spare key is hanging over there." He pointed to a row of three hooks on the wall next to the coat closet.

"Got it. Thanks again. I really appreciate you letting me crash here." She smiled again, and he decided he really needed to get the hell out of there.

"Okay then, see you later!" He grabbed his jacket from the closet and his phone and keys and took off.

After immersing himself in a few hours of strenuous outdoor work and driving his tractor around, Luke went into the winery to do some office work. He climbed the stairs to the upper level where he and his brothers and Hayden, and soon Brooke, had office space. Hayden's and Cam's offices were on one side, while Luke's and Jamie's were on the other. The middle area was broken up with a couple of offices, one of which would be Brooke's, space for future cubicles, and a conference room overlooking the vineyard.

As he approached his office, Jamie practically ran him down in the corridor.

"Hey, Luke, so, uh, I stopped by the house this morning."

Well, crap. He hadn't planned to keep Kelsey staying with him a secret, but neither had he meant to put her on the spot by having Jamie drop by unannounced. Furthermore, he didn't really want to talk about the situation. Best to just keep this to a minimum.

Luke didn't pause, just kept going to his office, knowing Jamie would follow him. "So you ran into Kelsey, then." He turned when he reached his desk. "She needed a place to crash for a few days, and I had a spare room. No big deal."

Ha, it *shouldn't* be a big deal, but it was wreaking havoc on his life. He couldn't stop thinking about her.

"Something wrong with her apartment?" Jamie asked.

Luke latched on to that excuse—her personal life and the reason she was staying with him weren't anyone's business unless she decided it was. "It has issues. She's actually looking to move. She'd been hoping to get Brooke's loft, but you beat her to it."

Jamie winced. "Oh, yikes. Well, now I feel bad. Is her place terrible?"

"Like I said, it has problems. She'll just keep looking."

"Are you sure? Because I could just come back to the house, I guess." He sounded disappointed, but Luke knew the offer was genuine.

"That's really cool of you, Jamie." Luke shook his head. "But don't worry about it. I know how much you love the loft."

Jamie smiled a bit sheepishly. "I really do. Reminds me a bit of my flat in London." He'd lived over there for a couple of years while going to the London School of Economics.

"That's great." Luke smiled at him as he sat down and opened his laptop, hoping Jamie would buy the clue and leave.

But he didn't. "So it seems like there's something between you and Kelsey, no?" He leaned against the doorframe and crossed his arms. "She's pretty cool."

They *were* kind of dating. Had at least been on a date or two, and she was coming to the wine dinner with him on Saturday. "There's…something. We're taking it pretty slowly. Just checking out the landscape."

Jamie nodded slowly. "Good plan. All right, then, I'll

leave you to it." He turned and left.

Luke scrubbed a hand over his face and read through his e-mail. Then his phone pinged.

Kelsey: *Wanted to let you know that you're out of milk. I can pick some up, but you'll likely beat me home.*

Home.

She'd called it home. It was a simple word, one that didn't necessarily mean anything except the place you planned to lay your head that night. How many times had he referred to a hotel room as home when on vacation? Why then did her usage of it give him a little jolt? A warmth that pressed into his chest and spread.

He responded to her, saying he'd pick some up. He wanted to ask how she'd slept, whether his bed was comfortable. Damn, imagining her in his bed was a thoroughly captivating image. The dark waves of her hair cascading over his pillow, her long, lithe legs tangled in his sheets… He needed to get a serious grip.

And get back to work.

He'd make himself so tired that he'd fall asleep long before she came home from work that night.

And there was that damn word again: home. Something about it evoked Kelsey. That had never happened with Paige. She'd mentioned moving in together several times, and he'd always balked. Somehow, Kelsey was different.

But how? It wasn't as if they'd been together a long time. Hell, he hadn't even made love to her yet.

Yet.

He dropped his head into his hands and stared, unseeing, at his desk. They were taking it slow all right. He just hoped he could survive it.

So Right

KELSEY RUSHED INTO Luke's house after working at the library on Saturday. She'd had to dash back to her apartment to pick up her dress and shoes for tonight. It was a warm fall day, and after running around—on foot—she needed a shower.

She glanced at the clock on the wall near the kitchen, saw that it was already five forty, and dumped her stuff to jump in the shower.

As she turned on the water, she thought about how she didn't remotely miss her apartment. In less than a minute, she'd step into nice hot water here, whereas at her apartment, she'd have to wait a good five minutes to reach a moderately warm temperature.

In three short days, Luke's house felt more like home than her apartment ever had. It wasn't hard to figure out why—the adorable bungalow was cozy and possessed several amenities her apartment didn't, such as the hot water heater from this century, a dishwasher, and a washer and dryer. The luxury of not having to go to the Laundromat was practically swoonworthy.

Then there was Luke's bed, which was about the most comfortable thing she'd ever slept on. And it smelled like him. It was, in a word, torture.

She stepped into the shower and quickly scrubbed up—she didn't have a lot of time. It was a good thing Luke was at the winery so she could run around half-naked as she got ready.

She'd barely seen him—they'd crossed paths briefly Thursday morning and then again this morning. She'd worked late the past two nights, which had probably been for the best. She wasn't sure she could handle spending time with him in these close quarters without taking things to the next level.

Why had she wanted this stupid no-sexy-times rule? Because she was trying to take this relationship—or whatever it was—slow. She liked Luke. A lot. But the specter of Noah, especially now that he was out of prison, loomed large in her mind.

Still, did that mean she couldn't have sex with Luke? Because, good Lord, she wanted to have sex with Luke.

But sex opened up the potential for new feelings and a deeper connection. She wasn't sure she was ready for that. Even if she wanted it.

Which she did. She was tired of being alone, she realized. And wasn't that a revelation?

She turned off the water and grabbed a towel to dry off. Wrapping it around herself, she padded from the bathroom to the living room where she'd left her dress draped over the back of the couch.

She didn't make it that far, however, because Luke was standing there staring at her. His gaze snapped to her face, but not before checking out her barely covered, still-damp body.

"I, uh, left my dress there." She inclined her head toward the couch, but Luke didn't follow her gaze.

"Yeah, you might need that." His gaze dipped again. He abruptly took a step back, as if to give her ample space to grab the dress.

She snapped her free hand out—the other was holding the towel in place because she didn't trust it to not fall away—and plucked her dress up. "I thought you were at the winery already."

"I was, but I had to come home to change." He was holding a garment bag, so she was confused.

"Those aren't your clothes?"

So Right

He looked momentarily dumfounded, then nodded. "Yes. I forgot my shoes. Work boots wouldn't look so great with my suit."

She couldn't wait to see him in a suit. Or in nothing. She swallowed.

"I was going to shower real quick," he said, finally averting his gaze. It seemed to take a great deal of effort. "Are you done in the bathroom?"

Now it was her turn to stare and say nothing. What had he said? All she could seem to process right now was that if he'd been a few minutes earlier, he could've joined her in the shower.

Oh, man, this was not good.

She jerked herself back to their pathetic attempt at a conversation. "Bathroom, yeah, I'm done." She turned and forced herself to walk to her bedroom. Her body didn't really want to move.

"So, uh, we can ride up to the winery together, then. Can you be ready in a half hour?"

That didn't give her a lot of time, but she hadn't needed to wash her hair again, thank goodness. She glanced back over her shoulder and took in his tousled hair, rugged jaw, and intensely dark eyes. "Sure. I'll hurry." Yep, couldn't wait to see him in that suit.

She took off for the bedroom and got ready as quickly as possible. She heard him shower and tried not to imagine him wet and hard and… *Never mind.* She let her imagination run rampant, and by the time she went to get her heels from the living room, she was ready to ask him to be late to the damn dinner. But of course he couldn't be. It was their first wine club event, was being catered by Hayden's brother and celebrity chef Kyle Archer, and would be attended by the customers who were putting their winery on the map.

Luke came out of the bathroom wearing crisp navy slacks and a white tee with his dress shirt thrown over it, still unbuttoned. Even though he wasn't "done," he looked so different out of his more casual clothes. "You, uh, left your clothes in the bathroom."

She blinked as she realized he was holding the clothing she was wearing before she'd showered. She'd completely forgotten about it. Wow, she had it bad. As she took the bundle from him, she thought of him collecting the various pieces, which included her bra and undies. Heat flamed her face. "Thanks."

He only nodded and then went into his room. She spun around and went to hers. Rather, his. She stood there and stared at his bed, which she'd made up very nicely that morning. But it needed a few throw pillows. And him. Lying across the throw pillows.

She put her clothes away and sat on the bed to put on her strappy heels. Then she stood and went to the mirror to finish her makeup. A few minutes later, Luke came to the open doorway.

He gave her a weak smile. "I don't suppose you can help me with my tie? I really suck at them."

"Of course." She'd tied plenty of Noah's. Not that she wanted to think about that just now. Or ever.

He stepped closer. He'd buttoned his white shirt to the collar, and the vibrant red-and-purple tie lay against the stiff cotton.

She couldn't help but get a huge whiff of his freshly showered scent, and the effect was a burst of heat that spread through her belly and much lower. It suddenly seemed as if she had fifty thumbs as she tried to grasp his tie.

"Looks like we planned our outfits," he said, keeping his chin up. "You look amazing."

Her dress was purple, so yeah, it did look like they'd coordinated. "We can pretend we're going to homecoming."

He laughed. "I don't have a corsage."

"We can stop and get one."

He started to shake his head, but seemed to think better of it since she was tying his tie. "No time." Something about his tone told her that if they *did* have extra time, he wouldn't waste it buying a corsage. Need, stark and hungry, pulsed between her thighs.

Her knuckles grazed his neck as she knotted the tie. She realized he was clean-shaven for the first time.

"You shaved."

His shoulder lifted slightly. "It seemed appropriate."

"I kind of like the stubble. Scratch that, I love the stubble."

He chuckled. "I get it—scratch that." He tipped his head down as she finished, and their eyes locked. "Duly noted."

More heat skittered up her spine. She smoothed her hand down the front of his tie. "All done."

"Not quite." He turned, and she followed, waiting for him in the area between their bedroom doors. He emerged again, shrugging into his navy coat. "Now I'm done. What do you think?"

She drank him in head to toe and clenched her hands into fists lest she pounce on him and ruin how great he looked. "I think I'm an idiot for insisting we keep our hands off each other."

Chapter Eleven
❦

WORDS JUMBLED IN Luke's brain but couldn't make the journey to his mouth, likely because other parts of his body were demanding to take over. He'd had a half erection since coming home to find her in a towel. No, that had been a full hard-on, which he'd managed to tame by thinking about the article he was writing for a local wine journal. Nothing like mildew and aphids to take the edge off your raging wood.

Except now the erection was back in full effect after what she'd said.

"Uh, we're kind of late here."

"Right. I know. Sorry, I wasn't suggesting anything." She looked away and went to grab her purse. "I'm ready."

She sure was. The front of her hair was pulled back so that the wavy locks hung down her back. Like him, she'd fancied up, wearing more makeup than normal. She looked sexy and seductive, especially when he took in the formfitting purple lace dress. He'd always known she was beautiful, but this was the closest he'd come to approximating how she looked under her clothing. He could hardly wait to see for himself. And maybe, just maybe, that would be soon based on what she'd said.

Down, boy, don't get ahead of yourself.

"Are you ready?" Her question dragged him back to the here and now.

"Yep." He pivoted and gestured for her to precede

him. "After you."

He grabbed his keys and locked the door on the way out. Then he held the car door for her.

She glanced up at him, her freshly glossed lips taunting him. "Thank you," she murmured.

He watched her legs, so sexy in those gorgeous black strappy sandals she was wearing, and after she was settled, closed the door.

On the way to the driver's seat, he tried to talk down his arousal. Damn, it was hard, especially when he climbed into the Jeep and got a fresh nose full of whatever scent she was wearing.

The air between them was so charged, he wondered if a fire might break out. He chuckled at the ridiculous thought as he started the engine.

"What?" she asked.

"Nothing."

"Really? You just laughed for no reason?"

He backed out of the driveway and cast her a sidelong glance. "You really want to know?"

She swallowed and looked away, and he threw the car into drive. They rode in silence for most of the ten-minute drive. As they approached the winery, she said, "You look really nice."

"Thanks."

"Like, *really* nice."

"Yeah, I got that based on what you said back at the house." Which he could hardly stop thinking about.

"I think I'm an idiot for insisting we keep our hands off each other."

Right now, it was taking everything he had not to touch her. But wait, their rule only included the house, didn't it? Right now, he could barely remember his name, let alone some asinine set of regulations they'd set up.

He pulled into the parking lot. Guests wouldn't be arriving for another half hour or so.

He turned off the car and jumped out to open her door. He helped her out, taking her hand and savoring the rush of exhilaration that raced through him. "Just to clarify. I can touch you now, right? Outside the house?"

"I don't think we ever decided that for certain." She glanced at where their fingers connected. "Like this?"

His lips curved into a smile. "I'll take what I can get."

She turned her hand, putting her palm against his and twining their fingers. Then she rested her other palm against his chest and leaned into him. "You can do more than that if you like."

His body surged with lust. "I would like very much." He tipped his head down to kiss her, but the sound of a car pulling into the lot drew them apart.

She let go of him and took a step back as Cam and Brooke parked next to them. Cam stepped out of the car and only spared them a brief look. "I see we're not the only ones running a bit late."

He rushed around to help Brooke get out of the car, and the four of them walked into the winery together.

Luke touched the small of Kelsey's back. "I need to help organize a few things. Grab a glass of wine if you want."

"Can I help with anything?"

He looked around. "I don't know. Maybe ask Brooke?" Cam had already disappeared into the kitchen.

Kelsey smiled up at him. "Sure. See you in a bit."

As people began to arrive, Luke went to the first wine tasting station on the bridge overlooking the vats.

Guests received their glasses when they checked in with Brooke and Bex, then made their way to Luke, who would pour chardonnay.

Kelsey appeared, joining him at the table where he was standing. "Brooke said I should come help you pour. That way you can focus on talking and answering questions."

He grinned, glad to have her as his companion. "Lucky me. I hope you're good with a wine opener."

"Good enough, though I'm sure you can teach me some moves." She was flirting with him again, and all he could think was how badly he wanted to kiss her.

He leaned toward her as the first group of guests approached. "You're going to kill me tonight. But it's going to be the best death."

She flashed him a smile as she picked up the bottle for the new arrivals. He talked to them about the chardonnay and about his vineyard management, answering any questions they had. As the group moved on, Luke took advantage of the moment to slip his hand along Kelsey's waist.

It felt so good to touch her. It was as if he'd crawled through a desert and had just found an oasis. He leaned close to her ear, barely resisting the urge to lick along the edge of her flesh. "You smell so fantastic." He felt her shiver.

She sidled closer to him, and he squeezed her waist. This night was going to take forever. And what would happen at the end? He could only hope she wanted what he did.

Liam and Aubrey came up then, and Luke poured wine into Liam's glass. Aubrey held up her water bottle with a sigh. "Sorry to miss out." She turned to Kelsey. "How are you doing?"

"Good, thanks."

Another few people joined them, and Luke started his spiel. They asked a few questions and then sipped their wine for a minute. He overheard Aubrey talking to Kelsey.

"I talked to the parole board, and he's in Washington now," Aubrey said, keeping her voice low.

Kelsey looked relieved. "That's great to hear."

Aubrey sipped her water. "I'll be in court first thing Monday for the restraining order. Sorry I wasn't able to get in there sooner. Don't worry, these things are a slam dunk in your case."

"Thanks so much for your help on this," Kelsey said, giving her a quick hug.

"It's my pleasure." She gave Kelsey a warm, earnest smile before joining her husband, and the group took off.

Luke took a step closer to Kelsey. "I couldn't help but overhear. Sounds like things are going well."

"As well as can be expected. I'm glad he's out of the state."

He heard the relief in her voice and wanted nothing more than to take her in his arms and hold her tight. "Me too."

George and her grandmother arrived at that moment, and Kelsey was delighted to see her. They embraced as Luke shook George's hand.

"Now this is a role reversal," George said, laughing. "You're serving me."

Luke grinned as he inclined his head toward Kelsey. "Actually, she's pouring."

Kelsey thrust the bottle at him. "Not this one."

Luke laughed and poured wine for both George and Ruby.

"How's it going with you two shacking up?" Ruby asked. Her eyes glinted with mischief, and Luke knew she was teasing.

Kelsey coughed, and Ruby handed her the wineglass. "You need a sip of this, dear."

Kelsey took that sip and gave it back. "Thank you. Things are fine." She sent a nervous glance toward George. "Uh, Noah's back in Washington now, so I'm feeling better about everything."

Ruby waved her hand. "I had to tell George about it. I hope you don't mind." She put her arm around George's waist and looked up at him, her gaze sparkling with something different now. "I'm afraid we aren't good at keeping secrets from each other."

George slid his arm around her shoulders and chuckled. "Afraid not." They were joined by more guests, and Luke did his thing. Then he and Kelsey were alone again for a brief moment.

He grabbed a bottle of water from the table and took a long drink before turning to Kelsey. "Is that okay with you? Your grandma telling George about all that? I have the sense you haven't told many people."

"It's weird, but I'm actually okay with it. Before this week, I think it would've bothered me because, yeah, I've kept it to myself for the most part." She glanced away, her gaze dipping to the tanks below them. "I'll admit...I was terrified when I got that text the other day, but knowing that I'm not alone helps." She looked at him again, and he took her hand.

"You are absolutely not alone."

Another group arrived, and it was a steady stream until dinner. He and Kelsey sat at a table with mostly people they didn't know, plus Luke's parents. It was a fun, raucous party, complete with crowd-pleasing thank-you speeches from both Cam and Hayden. Luke could've said something too, but preferred to stay out of the limelight.

Dad, who sat on Luke's right, leaned over and said, "Nice job tonight. Your mother and I are so proud." She was on Dad's other side and was chatting with the person on her right.

"Thanks, that means a lot."

"I, ah, I noticed you and Kelsey seem rather cozy."

Luke wondered if his dad was aware that they'd been intermittently holding hands under the table. He'd clearly caught the charged looks they'd been sharing. Shit, were they that obvious? "She's a great girl." What else was he supposed to say?

"Seems like it. Your mom would like to have you both to dinner soon. Should I deter her? I don't want to push you into something prematurely."

He wasn't sure if he was ready for dinner with the parents. "I'll let you know. We're taking things very slowly." And it was killing him.

Dad nodded. "I'll stave your mother off."

"Thanks, Dad, I appreciate that."

Dad clapped his shoulder. "You got it, son."

Dessert was served, and soon people began to get up. Luke leaned over to Kelsey. "I need to go help with the wine pickup." Some people had preordered cases, while others had bought wine tonight.

"Oh, I said I'd help take payments," she said. "I'll come along."

They'd set up a checkout area on the other side of the bridge, where they warehoused wine for club members. There was an exterior door there, which made wine pickup easy.

Kelsey sat with Brooke and Bex and took payments,

while Luke, Cam, Hayden, and Jamie filled the orders. Their half brother Dylan plus a few other Archers jumped in to help, which was much appreciated.

By eleven thirty it was down to just the principal wine folks and Kyle.

Luke collapsed into a chair in the tasting room along with everyone else. "I'm beat."

Bex kicked off her shoes and set her feet in Hayden's lap so he could massage them. "Try being six months pregnant." She let out a massive yawn.

"You guys should go," Cam said. "We'll take care of what's left."

"The hell with that," Luke said. "The rest can wait until tomorrow. Unless we need to handle any food situations in the kitchen." He looked over at Kyle.

Kyle shook his head. "Everything's put away and cleaned up. I had a good crew in there tonight." They'd hired some folks from The Arch and Vine and The Arch and Fox, the restaurant at the Archers' hotel, to help out. "I should get home. Maggie's going to need a break from Ripley." Their son was just over a month old. He clapped a hand on Hayden's shoulder on his way out. "Great event, little brother."

Hayden smiled. "Thanks."

Kyle took off, and Luke looked over at Kelsey who had her feet propped up on another chair. Those shoes were sexy as hell, but he imagined she couldn't wait to get them off. The question was whether she'd let him do the removing.

"So I guess we'll meet back here tomorrow to finish clean up?" Jamie asked.

Luke stood. "Yep. But don't expect me before noon." He went over to Kelsey and held out his hand. "Come on, gorgeous, let's hit the road."

She arched a brow at him, probably wondering why he'd called her that in front of everyone. He had nothing to hide. She was a beautiful woman, and he was completely under her spell. And he didn't really care who knew it.

She put her hand in his, and he pulled her to her feet. She winced, and he had his answer about the shoes.

Grabbing her purse, she cast a smile about the room. "Good night. Thanks for letting me help out."

"Thank *you* for helping," Cam said. "We'll lock up. Night, Luke."

"Night." Luke escorted Kelsey outside and then swept her into his arms.

"Luke! What are you doing? Put me down."

He carried her across the parking lot to his Jeep. "Not a chance, sweetheart. I saw your face—your feet are killing you. No surprise looking at your shoes. Sexy as hell, but not for standing like you did most of the night."

"Well, I didn't realize I'd be helping out like I did. But I enjoyed every minute."

He deposited her into the passenger seat. "I'm glad. Now take those shoes off, and I'll carry you into the house too."

He closed the door and rounded the car. Slowly. He wasn't looking forward to getting home where the hands-off rule was in effect. He was so sexually worked up, he thought he might explode.

Despite his snail's pace, he made it to the driver door and climbed inside. She already had her shoes off. A minute later, they were driving down the hill toward town.

"I had a really great time tonight," she said. It was dark, so he couldn't see much of her face. "I love listening to you talk about the vines and the grapes."

"Thanks. I loved having you there."

Silence reigned for a couple of minutes before she said, "I guess it's pretty obvious we're dating."

"Probably." He let the word out slowly. "Is that okay?"

"Yes. In fact, I was hoping we could talk about that."

He tensed as he pulled onto Main Street and drove through town. "What do you mean?"

"When I agreed to come stay with you, I was nervous about how it would affect our relationship. Or whatever it is we have going on. I didn't want it to accelerate things." She paused. "I'm still…hesitant."

The tension inside him released, but it wasn't relief. It was disappointment. Not with her, with himself for stupidly allowing his hopes to get out of hand.

"I understand. You're still welcome to stay with me as long as you like, and we'll keep our relationship—or whatever it is—in check."

He turned onto his street.

"I'm not being very clear. Sorry."

He tensed again as he drove into the driveway and parked the car. "What do you mean?" He looked over at her, and the porch light cast its glow across her face as she turned toward him.

"I mean I want to repeal the no-sexy-times rule. Immediately. If you're okay with that."

The lust he'd worked so hard to quell all night came roaring to a head, making his body thrum with need. Anticipation coursed through him as he looked her in the eye. "I've never been more okay with anything in my entire life."

Chapter Twelve

꒰ ꒱

IT WAS TEMPTING to throw herself into his lap, but Kelsey waited for him to come around the Jeep and help her out of the car. She picked up her purse and shoes as he swung the door open. Then he picked her up as if she weighed nothing and she twined her arms around his neck. He shut the door with his foot and carried her to the house.

He stopped on the porch. "Crap, I have to set you down to unlock the door."

"I can do it. Keys in your pocket?" At his nod, she reached into his pants and pulled out his keys. Her hand grazed the steel of his erection.

"Um, a little to the right?" he urged.

She smiled as she reached over and unlocked the door. He pushed inside and set her down, then shut the door and locked it. That was pretty much all she could stand.

Dropping her shoes and purse over the back of the couch, she stood on her toes to kiss him. He met her more than halfway. He wrapped his arms around her and lifted her against his chest, his mouth plundering hers in desperate abandon.

She hiked up her dress and wrapped her legs around his waist. He groaned and carried her forward, taking her in the direction of the bedroom. His bedroom.

Once he'd reached his destination, she unwrapped her legs from him and slid down his body.

He pulled his mouth from hers. "Why'd you do that?" His lips tracked along her jaw.

She pushed his coat from his shoulders, and he shrugged it to the floor. "To undress you, silly." She tugged at the knot of his tie and loosened the fabric, then pulled it free. She went to work unbuttoning his shirt. "Although I sort of hate to do that, because you look so damn hot. Please find another reason to dress up soon."

"I will wear this every day if it turns you on."

After she had all his buttons free, she rubbed her hand against his face and kissed him briefly before tugging on his lower lip with her teeth. "And don't shave. I like the scruff."

"Right, you said that. I'll never shave again," he rasped, claiming her mouth in a heart-stopping kiss.

She drew away long enough to say, "Never say never. Honestly, you're sexy without it too."

He kissed along her throat, and she cast her head back. "If you're trying to seduce me, allow me to let you in on a secret: I'm a sure thing."

She laughed, tangling her fingers in his hair. "I should've realized that earlier. The way you were looking at me… I was certain my clothes would melt off."

"Now that's a superhero trait I wouldn't mind." He licked the spot just beneath her ear, causing her to shiver. "Alas, I'm going to have to do this the old-fashioned way. And as much as I hate to divest you of this incredibly sexy dress, it's kind of in my way." His fingers found the zipper at her back and eased it down, exposing her flesh.

She retaliated by pushing his shirt off and reaching for his belt buckle.

He arched a brow at her. "Oh, we're going for that now, are we?"

She lifted a shoulder and gave him a saucy stare. "Seems fair."

He growled just before he kissed her again. This one was hotter and wetter than the others. It stoked the fire within her until she was moaning into his mouth. His hands dove beneath the open back of her dress and massaged her flesh. His fingers flicked at her bra strap until it came loose.

She whipped his belt off with a whoosh and cast it aside. Then she felt for the button on his pants. Her knuckles grazed his erection through the fabric, and she got distracted. She rubbed her hand against him as desire pulsed through her.

His hips came forward, pressing into her hand, and she increased her pressure. He backed away from the kiss and pushed her dress off her shoulders. She helped him pull it down and shimmied out of it before kicking it aside. He swept her bra off, tossing it away, then brought his hands up to cup her breasts.

The second he touched her, she closed her eyes and moaned. He flicked her nipples lightly, then massaged them with what felt like the pad of his thumbs. Sensation pooled and built from those peaks, sending wild desire arcing through her. Then there was heat and moisture. Her eyes flew open. He was bent over her, his mouth and tongue teasing her breast.

She arched back but couldn't keep herself upright. She turned and fell back on the bed, taking him with her.

He wrapped his arms around her and broke her fall against the mattress. He landed beside her instead of crushing her with his weight. He'd moved quickly, thoughtfully. And now purposefully as he rose over her and rededicated his attention to her breasts. His mouth tantalized one while his fingers pulled and played with the other. He was focused and intense, stirring a pleasure she'd never experienced. She hadn't realized this sort of foreplay could drive her so close to an orgasm, but that was exactly how it felt.

Heat flooded her core, and she pivoted her hips toward him, seeking his touch, seeking release. His hand skimmed down her abdomen, stoking her arousal to even greater heights. He found the edge of her underwear and tugged them down. She wriggled her hips to help him, and a moment later, she lay nude beside him.

But he was still wearing pants. And a T-shirt. She pushed at him and turned so that she could grasp the hem. The position was awkward, but she didn't have to do much. He sat up and pulled the garment over his head, then threw it across the room.

"Pants, please," she said, her voice husky and dark.

He rolled to his back and unzipped his fly while toeing off his shoes. She grasped the waistband and tugged it down his thighs, but abandoned her effort when he leaned down to pull the pants off completely and remove his socks. As soon as he lay back, she snagged his boxer briefs and drew them down, exposing his flesh, her gaze riveted on his hard shaft. It sprang free when the briefs were low enough, and she didn't wait to reach out and touch it, her fingers curling around him.

"God. Kelsey. Just…wait." He moaned and then gasped, his breath coming harder as she worked her hand along his length.

"Hmm. No, afraid I can't." She smiled to herself as

his hips moved in response to her touch.

He managed to get his underwear off despite her unwavering attention. With another low growl, he flipped her to her back and came over her. His mouth came down on hers hard, but she loved every second of it as his tongue plunged into her mouth. It was a fierce coupling, a desperate exchange, as she strained up to press herself to him in any way that she could.

She clasped his hips and pulled him between her legs. His cock was hot against her, thrilling her. "Condom?" she asked between kisses.

His body went still, and he retreated from her. Cool air rushed over her as the space between them grew. She propped herself up on her elbows. "What's wrong?"

He sat back on his haunches. "Is this…too fast? I don't want to rush you."

"You aren't."

"You were hesitant before, and while I recognize we have some crazy chemistry going on, I don't want you to have any regrets."

Kelsey scrambled up, kneeling before him. She touched his smooth cheek, her fingertips caressing his soft flesh. "I won't." She leaned forward and kissed him, her lips gently suckling his. She pulled back, smiling at him. "I love that you're the cool head of reason. That means more to me than you know. I'm ready for this. I want you. If you want me too."

He cupped her face and kissed her, his tongue playing sweetly with hers as he smoothed her hair back from her cheekbones. "I want you more than I've ever wanted anyone."

A giddy burst of warmth exploded in her chest. "Really?"

He laughed softly. "Honest to God." He kissed her again, this time with more heat and urgency. He caressed her breast, tugging briefly on the nipple before descending between her legs and finding her clit. His touch was soft at first, teasing, then more insistent as his fingers dragged over her cleft.

She clutched his shoulders and rode his hand, her hips moving as he pushed her toward release. It had been so long since she'd orgasmed with someone...and she was so close.

He left her mouth and kissed a trail to her breast, where he licked and sucked her nipple, drawing forth a guttural moan from her as pleasure spiraled through her. His hand worked faster, his fingers slipping inside her now, filling her, then going back to her clit. She held on for dear life as he coaxed her body to shuddering new heights.

"I can't." Her knees buckled, and he guided her back to the bed.

He drew on her nipple, pulling, as ecstasy raced over her. He thrust his fingers into her. "Scream for me, Kelsey."

He didn't have to ask twice. She arched off the bed as she came, crying out, heedless of how she sounded. He soothed her through the release, and then he was gone. Mindless, she lay there panting, her body aquiver. That had been...life changing.

He came back between her legs, and she opened her eyes to see he was wearing a condom.

"Just so you know, I'm clean," she said. "But I'm not on any birth control. Sorry. I didn't have a reason."

"Don't apologize." He bent forward and kissed her. "I'm clean too."

She reached between them and clasped the base of

his cock. He thrust into her hand. She parted her legs wider and bent them at the knee as she guided him to her sheath. He slid into her, and she let her head fall back, her eyes closing. She was so sensitive from before, and now it felt as though she was going to have another orgasm, which had never happened to her before. White lights danced behind her eyelids. He slipped in deeper, filling her. She let her legs fall open, laying herself bare to him, and brought her knees up even higher. The intensity of his invasion grew to an intoxicating height so that she thought she might burst.

Then he moved, and she quite simply fell apart. Another orgasm, more powerful than the first, washed over her. She clutched at his hips and arched up against him. He drove into her again and again, and it was absolute bliss. She'd never felt such acute pleasure.

He didn't let up, relentlessly pulsing into her until she heard him groan. She ran her hands up and down his back. "Yes, come with me," she urged.

He yelled her name and buried himself deep inside her. She held him tight, smiling. Minutes later, he gently rolled away. She reached for him.

"I'll be right back," he said softly before pressing his lips to hers. Then he left the bed, and she heard him in the bathroom. She pulled the covers back and burrowed between the sheets.

A minute later, he came and slipped in behind her. She scooted backward, and he wrapped his arm around her to hold her close to his chest.

She lifted his hand to her mouth and pressed a kiss to the back. "Thank you. That was a first for me— multiple orgasms."

"Really?" He sounded surprised but also a bit proud. As he should be.

She grinned. "Really."

He kissed her temple, her cheek, the shell of her ear. His heat and strength seeped into her, and she fell asleep smiling, thinking she hadn't felt this protected—this *safe*—in years.

Actually, she'd never felt that ever.

♥ ♪

IT TOOK LUKE a moment to realize the soft, warm body against his wasn't a dream and that last night had been real too. He turned to his side and inhaled the fruity scent of Kelsey's hair. Pushing the dark curls aside, he pressed a kiss to her neck—that tender, delicious spot just beneath her ear.

She lay on her side, her back to him, as she let out a small sigh that brought his cock fully erect. He scooted closer, spooning her from behind. She bent slightly at the waist, gently thrusting the sweet curve of her ass against his erection. Lust jolted through him, and he slipped his hand over her hip, lightly caressing her flesh as he moved up to cup her breast. Her nipple hardened with the barest touch. She had to be awake now, but her eyes were still closed.

He pinched the nipple, pulling it before gentling his ministrations. Her breathing picked up and her lips parted. Definitely awake.

He trailed his fingertips down over her belly, grazing her pelvis as he found the sweetest spot between her legs. She opened her thighs, giving him better access and he slipped his finger into her cleft. She was hot and wet, and his cock was throbbing. He could slide into her from behind right now and bring them both to easy ecstasy. But last night had been her first experience with multiple orgasms, and she'd seemed so…happy. He wanted to do that for her again.

He ducked under the covers and clasped her hip, pressing it down to the mattress. He stroked her clit as he rolled over her leg, settling himself between her thighs. It was relatively dark, but he didn't need to see. Only to taste and feel. He licked at her folds, and she arched up, gasping. Her fingers tangled in his hair.

"Luke!"

He smiled against her before suckling her flesh and burying his tongue deep inside her. She cried out, her legs falling open to encourage his mouth. He pulled her thighs over his shoulders and spread her with his fingers. She bucked up and let out a series of pants and moans that were the most erotic sounds he'd ever heard. His cock strained against the bed, and he could barely wait to lose himself inside her.

He pulled his mouth from her and used his hand to massage her flesh and his fingers to thrust into her. She moved with him, fucking him, and he could sense that she was close. He tongued her again and pressed on her clit. A rush of moisture was his reward as she came hard against his mouth.

He pushed the covers back and licked up her abdomen. Her harsh pants filled the room. She clutched at him, and he clasped her knees, pulling them and pushing them wide as he positioned himself between her thighs. She grasped his cock, her hand tightening around the base. He sucked in a breath.

"Kelsey, I'm so close."

She slitted her eyes at him, and he'd never seen a sexier sight—her dark hair spread over the pale gray pillow, her pink lips parted in desire. "Good." She stroked his shaft and used her thumb to flick the tip. Her eyes opened wider. "Um, condom, please."

Shit, he'd almost forgotten. Amateur move. He left her briefly to grab a condom from the bedside table. She reached over and snatched it from his fingertips, then opened it with her teeth. He'd never wanted to be a condom wrapper until that moment.

She rolled the condom over his cock, turning a mundane task into something unbelievably sensual. He groaned and nudged at her opening. She guided him in, and he drove hard and fast. He slid his hands up to her thighs, holding them as he thrust into her. She cast her head back, crying out.

"Tell me you're coming again," he rasped.

She made a cacophony of those delicious, erotic sounds. "Almost."

He reached down and stroked her clit. "How about now?"

She made a high, keening sound, and he had his answer. He drover harder and deeper into her, feeling his own orgasm building. It might not be more than one, but if it was anything like last night, it was going to be epic.

Her muscles continued to contract around him, and he lost sense of time and space, his body simply moving with need. Ecstasy flooded him, and he cried out her name.

She moved with him as he came, her muscles clenching around him, taking everything he had to give. When he could think coherently again, he opened his eyes a fraction and saw her lithe body still arching with him. He stroked her abdomen, loving the silky feel of her. Then he massaged her breasts, lightly tweaking her nipples. She squeaked and opened her eyes. "Aren't you done?"

He let out a low chuckle. "For now. That doesn't mean you have to be." He wanted to bring her to orgasm again and again. Maybe all day.

She looked over at the clock on his bedside table. "Unfortunately, I do. We slept kind of late, and I need to shower and get to the library."

Damn, that put a damper on his plans. "There's no one else who can work for you?"

"Afraid not. My assistant isn't scheduled today, and I think she's busy anyway."

He exhaled in disappointment. "Can I at least make you breakfast while you shower?"

She smiled. "That I will take you up on." She rolled away from him and nodded toward the condom. "Go do your thing first."

He stood and walked toward the bathroom.

"And, hey, can I have a rain check?" she called after him.

He looked back over his shoulder, grinning in anticipation. "Absolutely."

She licked her lips, and he groaned before heading into the bathroom.

After pulling on some athletic shorts and a loose T-shirt, he headed into the kitchen to make some eggs and sausage. He hoped she liked sausage. And eggs. These were important things he really ought to know. He looked forward to learning every little thing about her.

Just as he was about to throw the eggs into the skillet, there was a knock on the door. Who the hell would be coming by on a Sunday morning? Maybe Jamie had forgotten something else.

Luke wiped his hands on a towel and jogged to the

door. He opened it and froze. Standing on the threshold was the last person he'd expected to see.

"Paige."

She smiled, and he realized he'd forgotten her dimples. "Luke!" She sprang forward and wrapped her arms around him. Then she kissed his cheek, her mouth lingering against his flesh.

He took a step back and noticed that her gaze was fixed behind him and to the right. Toward the bathroom where Kelsey had been drying her hair and probably hadn't heard the door. He realized—too late—that the sound of the blow dryer had stopped.

Well, shit.

He spun around and saw Kelsey's wide-eyed stare just before she recovered.

He needed to think fast, but he couldn't seem to come up with words.

Damn it.

Except curse words. Those were coming at him in a deluge.

He took a few steps toward Kelsey, putting more space between him and Paige. "Uh, Kelsey, this is Paige. Paige, this is Kelsey—my girlfriend."

Kelsey's gaze locked with his for a moment, and her eyes widened again, though more subtly than before.

Paige stalked forward and offered Kelsey her hand. "Hi, I'm Luke's ex. He didn't tell me about you when I talked to him the other day. Silly boy." She laughed and cast him a dark look that didn't match the jovial response.

Kelsey's mouth pulled into a tight smile. "Oh, well, he didn't tell me you were coming for a visit either. I guess his memory isn't the best. Anyway, I need to get to work." She went to the couch and grabbed her purse. "Bye."

She left before Luke had a chance to salvage the situation.

Fuck fuck fuckity fuck.

Yep, he had plenty of swearwords.

Finally regaining his senses, he ran to the door and dashed outside, just barely catching Kelsey before she drove off. "Wait," he said as he jogged up to her passenger window.

She pursed her lips and waved him off.

He shook his head and knocked on the window.

After a pause, she rolled down the window. "What?"

"I'm really sorry. Can we talk about this?"

She glanced at the clock on her dash. "I need to get to the library."

"You have a few minutes. You were going to eat, after all."

"Luke, I can't do this right now. Last night was…a big step for me. And to have this thrown at me this morning—" She turned her head away from him.

"I had no idea she was coming."

She looked at him again, and her eyes were sad. "It doesn't matter. You need to go deal with that. Listen, I wasn't sure if I was ready for a relationship, and I'm definitely not ready for a guy with baggage."

Goddammit. He ran his hand through his hair, growing frustrated. "There's no baggage."

She tossed an irritated look toward the house. "I'd beg to differ. Please let me go."

Frowning, he took a step back. "We'll talk later."

She rolled up the window and backed out of the driveway. As he watched her leave, he wondered why she was even taking her car since the library was only a few blocks away. Maybe she didn't plan to come back after work.

A cavalcade of curse words marched through his brain. He turned and stalked into the house, slamming the door after he got inside.

Paige had doffed her jacket and set her purse down and was now stirring eggs on the stove. She smiled brightly. "Can't let good eggs go to waste. I always loved your scrambled eggs."

Seriously? "You think I want to have breakfast with you after that?"

She shrugged. "You have to eat. So what's the story? You didn't tell me you had a girlfriend."

"Because I didn't when I talked to you. This is new." So damn new it might not even count as official. "You also know how much I value my privacy."

Her face fell, and he could see that she was disappointed. "I see."

"Paige, I don't know what you were thinking would happen by surprising me, but we're over. We've been over for a long time."

She pulled the eggs from the stove and served them onto the plates he'd gotten out of the cupboard. "Only because you live here, and I lived in California. But I have a job interview tomorrow. It looks promising. We had a phone interview last week, and we really hit it off."

"I'm happy for you. But you moving up here isn't going to change things." While he'd relied on the excuse of the geographical distance for the growing rift in their relationship, he'd also told her he thought it was for the best that they break up.

She dished up the sausage, which she'd also apparently finished cooking while he'd been outside. "How do you know it won't change things? If we're together, things might go back to the way they were."

How could she want that? They'd been happy for a while, but the clingier she'd become, the more he'd pushed her away. She wanted their relationship to progress, and the more she'd told him that, the farther he'd wanted to run. "I don't want things to go back to the way they were."

She'd carried the plates to the table while he'd been thinking and now folded her arms over her chest. "Right. That would be too much effort. I wonder if Kelsey is aware of how little you like to contribute to a relationship."

"If that's how you feel, why are you here?"

She dropped her arms to her sides and came toward him, stopping far too close for his comfort. "Because I still love you, Luke, isn't that obvious? I've tried to move on, but I can't." She looked away from him, and he could see that she was truly hurting.

Damn and damn.

His ire faded. "I'm sorry. Really. But I can't change the way I feel."

When she looked at him again, some of the fire had returned to her eyes. "I hope you'll be honest with Kelsey. She deserves to know that you have issues with intimacy. Or whatever it is. Don't let her fall head over heels in love with you while you're thinking you'd rather just be fuck buddies."

"Hey, you meant more to me than that."

"Did I? I'd thought so—once. But now I'm not so sure." She picked up her jacket and purse. "If you ever felt something for me, please be honest with Kelsey. Or maybe I should tell her what you're really like."

The irritation he'd just quashed flared into anger. "Don't threaten me. I never took you for nasty."

She averted her gaze again. "I'm not. I'm...sorry." She shook her head and sent him a sad look. "Tell Kelsey the truth so she can go into this with her eyes open. You owe her that much." She turned and went to the door. "See you, Luke."

Literally, if she was going to be working up here. And wouldn't that be awkward as hell?

"Hey, where's your interview tomorrow? Maybe I can put in a good word." He might be annoyed with her, but at the end of the day, they'd had good times together and he didn't wish her ill.

"Bellwether—in Salem."

A good half hour plus away. Yay. "Hmm, I don't know anyone, but I can ask around."

"Only if you want. I appreciate it, thanks." She opened the door, and he walked over to see her out.

"Good luck, Paige."

She gave him a last, longing look before turning and going to her rental car parked in the street.

Luke closed the door and leaned against it. That had been an absolute disaster. He wanted desperately to talk to Kelsey, but Paige's words weighed heavy on him.

Did he have issues with intimacy? He knew she meant closeness in a romantic relationship and not just sex. But the sex was a red flag. There'd been an occasion when Paige had asked him to make love to her. Those two words had frozen him—he'd realized in that moment that he didn't love her, not the kind of love she deserved, and wasn't sure he ever would. From then on, he'd started to distance himself from her.

Would the same thing happen with Kelsey? He couldn't know. He hoped not. He cared about her so very much. The thought of feeling that way about her, or rather, *not* feeling that way made him queasy. He tried to think back and recall if he'd felt that way at the start with Paige. She was the longest relationship he'd ever had. He'd dated someone in college for a year or so, but they'd never been serious.

Apprehension wove through him. He'd been angry with the way Paige had shown up without warning and her feeble attempt at blackmail, but he'd also seen her hurt. He hadn't meant to cause her pain. When he thought about inadvertently doing that to Kelsey after she'd already suffered so much…

He closed his eyes and knocked his head back against the door. After a few minutes, he took a deep breath and went to the kitchen to clean up the breakfast he no longer felt like eating.

He stalked to the bedroom and took in the rumpled sheets. Memories of last night and this morning rushed over him, sparking his desire for Kelsey—both physically and emotionally. He had no idea where they were going, but he wanted to find out.

Chapter Thirteen
♡ ⚘

FORTUNATELY, THE FIRST half of Kelsey's shift flew by, thanks in part to a five-year-old who'd wanted to have her birthday party at the library. They'd set up in the children's nook, and Kelsey had read three books of the birthday girl's choosing. It had been a welcome diversion after the craptasticness of the morning.

Craptasticness?

As a librarian, she was supposed to be good with words. Hopefully that included making them up.

She shook her head, thinking she was more of a mess than she'd thought. And damn, was she a mess. Last night—and this morning—had been so fantastic, and then, in the blink of an eye, it had all gone to crap.

Yep, craptasticness was her new favorite made-up word.

Her phone buzzed again. She looked at it vibrating on the counter in front of her. Tempting as it was to pick it up, she was certain it was Luke. He'd already texted her at least four times, asking if he could pick her up after work, asking if she had time to talk, asking if she was ignoring him.

No. No. Yes.

She'd actually driven her car this morning, which was ridiculous since she'd had to park it almost as far away as she would've walked from Luke's house. But there was something far more dramatic about stalking out of a scene like this morning and getting in a car to drive away. Merely walking down an idyllic street lined with trees turning red and gold just didn't send the right message.

Had she been trying to send a message?

She had no idea. She'd been surprised and hurt and disappointed. And scared. She knew, of course, that relationships didn't come with guarantees. She'd been in a relationship that had pretty much scared her off relationships forever. Or so she'd thought.

Luke challenged everything she thought she knew. He was kind, considerate, sexy as hell, and so caring. But it was all so new. This morning had proven that. Apparently, his ex still thought she had a shot with him.

Kelsey had come out of the bathroom and nearly tripped when she'd seen Paige's arms around Luke. Then she'd kissed his cheek, and Kelsey's gut had twisted. There was plenty of jealousy, but also anger. She'd let down her guard and gotten kicked in the face for her trouble.

She straightened her shoulders. Time to stop wallowing and get back to work. She picked up the books she'd just unboxed from yesterday's late mail delivery and took them to the Spanish-language display she was creating. There were a lot of migrant workers in the area, and Kelsey hoped to encourage them to come to the library. Her Spanish wasn't great, but she was working on making some signs and flyers and had an old college friend in Washington who was fluent who would ensure she got them right.

An older gentleman who'd been browsing the nonfiction area walked by her on his way to the door. "Don't know why you need those books."

She smiled at him as she propped a picture book on

the table. "We have a good-sized Spanish-speaking population in the county. I'm sure they'd love to come in and find books in their language."

He scoffed. "They need to learn English if they want to live here."

Kelsey's adrenaline spiked. She didn't want to have an ugly confrontation, but this guy was a jerk. "They do learn English. They also want to hold on to their culture. I think that's great. America is a melting pot, after all."

He rolled his eyes. "You young people and your PC garbage." He turned and left while Kelsey stared after him.

A couple in their thirties walked up to her. "We overheard your conversation," the woman said. "You were amazing for standing up to him."

Kelsey began to relax. "Thanks. I just couldn't let him say that."

"We would've backed you up if he'd kept on," the man said, returning her smile. "Good job. And we love the library."

She'd seen them in here before, usually on Sundays, she realized. "Thanks. I appreciate hearing that. Anything I can help you find today?"

"Actually, we're looking for a documentary. It doesn't look like you have it, but maybe it's checked out."

"I can certainly look. And I can try to find a copy at another library too." She turned toward the counter. "Come with me."

Kelsey immersed herself in work until it was just about closing time. As she eyed the clock, she wondered what she was going to do after she left. Go back to Luke's? She still wasn't ready to talk to him. Go home? She could…but more and more, she loathed the idea of spending time there at all. It was just so small and dingy, and after the water pressure at Luke's house, she thought she might cry if she had to shower at her apartment.

Pulling her phone from her pocket, she texted Gram and asked if she had dinner plans. A few minutes later, Gram responded with an enthusiastic invitation for her and Luke to come eat at George's with her. Kelsey accepted without bothering to clarify that it would just be her.

At last it was closing time, and she went to the door to flip the sign and lock up. As she got there, the door pushed open, and all she could see was a giant bouquet of flowers.

Luke's head popped out from behind it, and he gave her a smile that normally would've melted her socks. However, her gaze went back to the flowers and stayed. Anxiety curled inside her, and ice chilled her spine.

"I brought you these," he said, holding them out. "I wanted to apologize—*profusely*—for what happened this morning."

She stared at the flowers but didn't take them. She couldn't. She *wouldn't*.

Her heart threatened to beat out of her chest. She felt as though she couldn't breathe. Turning, she went to the counter where she had her purse locked up in the cabinet. Her hands were shaking, but she pulled the key from her pocket.

"Kelsey?" He'd followed her. "Are you just going to pretend I'm not here?" He lowered his hand and let the flowers drop so that they pointed to the ground.

"No," she said slowly, unlocking the cabinet. "I don't have anything to say."

"Then you can just listen. Paige is the girlfriend I mentioned to you before. We dated for a few years when I lived in California. Then we tried a long-distance relationship, but it didn't work out. I guess she's still sort of hung up on me. I didn't realize, and I had no idea she was coming this morning. I'm so sorry."

Kelsey put her purse over her shoulder. "I understand."

He frowned. "It doesn't sound like it."

She walked toward the door. "Luke, I'm on my way out."

Again, he followed her. "Kelsey, we need to talk about this. Please?"

He was probably right, but she couldn't do it now. Not with those god-awful flowers. "I can't right now."

"You couldn't this morning either. When would it be convenient?"

She heard the edge to his tone and pivoted to face him. "I'm sorry this isn't convenient for you. But I don't owe you *anything*." She refused to feel beholden to anyone ever again. Not after Noah. Not after feeling as though her life wasn't her own.

He winced. "I'm sorry. I'm just frustrated. We had such a nice night and morning, and now it's all...a mess." He held the flowers out to her again. "Can I at least give you these?"

"No. You can burn them." She opened the door. "Please go, I need to lock up."

He stared at her, and she glanced away, unable or maybe unwilling to look at the hurt in his gaze. Then he turned and walked out. He paused on the sidewalk and waited for her to lock the door. "Will I see you later?"

She pulled her purse strap higher on her shoulder as she stuffed the keys in one of the pockets. "I don't know. I'll…text. Or something. Bye."

She spun around and strode away, feeling his stare burn into her back.

The late afternoon sun was bright and crisp, the breeze light and cool as she made her way to her car. Once inside, she sat there and stared at the park where children played, and a couple sat on a blanket enjoying a picnic. It was an idyllic scene and yet all she could see were the flowers Luke had brought her.

God, she hated flowers. How many times had Noah shown up with an apology, an excuse, and a goddamn bouquet? More times than she cared to remember. It had gotten to the point that the mere smell of lilies or freesia or carnations or, worst of all, roses sent her into a panic. Even now, her heart was still pounding and her mouth was dry.

She started the car and headed toward George's. Gram had texted her the address. It was south of town—just a short eight or so minute drive. On the way, she did her meditative breathing, and by the time she arrived, her pulse had returned to normal.

Kelsey parked behind Gram's car in the driveway. She stared at the house for a minute. It was a very nice Craftsman style. It was fairly new, and she wondered if he'd had it built. She knew he owned several acres of vineyard, which stretched up a gentle slope behind the house.

Gram came out onto the front porch and Kelsey stepped out of her car. "Are you coming in or not?" Gram asked, smiling.

A sense of peace stole over Kelsey. She was so grateful to have her grandmother here. "I'm coming."

So Right

She locked the car and went up to the porch, where she hugged Gram tight.

Gram patted her back. "My goodness. You act as though you haven't seen me in ages. I just saw you last night."

"I know. It's just… It's been a rough day." Between the ex-girlfriend, the obnoxious patron, and the flowers, perhaps rough wasn't a severe enough word. She backed away and tried to summon a smile but failed.

Gram put her arm around her shoulders. "Come inside and let's see if George can't make you one of his signature margaritas."

"He doesn't have to tend bar on his day off," Kelsey said as she opened the door.

Gram chuckled. "Just try and stop him."

Gram closed the door behind them as Kelsey took in the entry, which led to a massive great room. Tall windows on the opposite wall climbed probably twenty feet, nearly to the ceiling. The view of the vineyard was expansive—and breathtaking.

"George, your home is beautiful." It was, in fact, very tastefully appointed and looked like it belonged in a magazine spread.

"Isn't it?" Gram said. "He hired a decorator. Can you believe that?"

George laughed as he came from the left, where a massive island separated the kitchen from the great room. "I spent my entire life in the military. What the hell did I know about decorating a house?" He grinned at Kelsey. "What can I get you to drink?"

"I think she needs a margarita," Gram said. "She's had a bad day."

George's brow furrowed. "That's no good. Come on

in and sit down at the bar. I'll whip up something tasty." He winked at her and went into the large gourmet kitchen.

Kelsey looked around in disbelief as she made her way to one of the cushy leather barstools. "George, I still can't believe you live here, like this. I never would've guessed this place belonged to a retired marine."

"I think that's exactly what Ruby said." He looked at Gram. "You want a margarita too, sweetheart?"

Sweetheart? Kelsey perked up. She knew they were spending a lot of time together but wasn't sure how serious their relationship had gotten. She should've paid closer attention at the wine dinner last night. Except she'd been too wrapped up in Luke.

And there went her mood again.

George poured three margaritas. "I don't blend 'em here at Casa Wilson. I can't remember which you prefer, Kelsey."

"I don't have a preference. On the rocks is fine by me."

"Excellent." He finished and handed one to Kelsey and then one to Gram, who'd sat down beside her. Then he picked up the third and offered a toast. "To getting to spend an evening with two of the most beautiful women in the world. I'm a lucky old bastard." There was a twinkle in his eye as he sipped his margarita.

Kelsey took a long drink and set the glass back on the granite countertop. "George, you make a mean margarita."

"Thank you, and it's my pleasure. Now tell us about your lousy day."

Oh man, did she really want to? She didn't see a way

to avoid it, so she told them about the jerk at the library.

George shook his head. "I run into guys like that around here from time to time. Like you, I have no trouble setting them straight. Well done, Kelsey, I'd say your family did a good job raising you." He tossed a warm smile at Gram.

Kelsey preferred to steer the topic away from herself. "So, it, uh, looks like you two are pretty cozy. Do you need a chaperone?"

Gram and George laughed, and Kelsey smiled as she took another sip of her drink.

"I think we're a little past chaperones, dear," Gram said. "But yes, I think cozy is a nice description. Rather like you and Luke." She arched her brows at Kelsey as her lips curved up. "Except you've done us one better since you're living together. I hope you're not rushing into anything. Especially after what you went through with Noah."

So much for trying to deflect the conversation away from her. Kelsey glanced at George to see his reaction. How much had Gram told him about Noah?

"Rest easy, Kelsey. Your secrets are safe with me. I'm a professional—used to work for the CIA."

Kelsey's jaw dropped. "Seriously?"

George nodded. "I'd rather you kept that to yourself. It's not something I advertise. For perhaps obvious reasons."

Kelsey could think of several, first and foremost being his safety—and the safety of those around him. "Do I need to worry about Gram being with you?"

He chuckled again, a low, warm sound. "Nah. That was a long time ago now. I'm an old bartender. Nobody cares about me."

Gram gave him a loving—yes, loving—look. "*I* care."

"I know." He blew her a kiss.

Kelsey took another drink of her margarita and marveled at how adorable they were and how thrilled she was to see Gram so happy. She was also quite pleased that the conversation had turned again.

But that was short-lived.

"Back to you and Luke," Gram said, turning toward Kelsey on the stool. "Are you taking things slow?"

She considered answering yes and just leaving it at that. However, she'd realized after Gram had come to town that she didn't like being alone. Noah had isolated her from family and friends, and it had taken her far too long to realize that she missed having people in her life.

"Sort of," she said softly. "I like him a lot. But I'm… I'm not sure I'm ready for a relationship."

Gram clasped her hand over Kelsey's on the counter. "I think it's good that you're cautious."

"I don't know," George said, drawing both Kelsey and Gram to look at him. "If there's anything I've learned, it's that life is short. It took me over six decades to realize I wanted someone in my life. I never wanted to worry about someone else. I couldn't, really, not in my profession."

It made sense to Kelsey that he wouldn't want to have relationships. But it wasn't the same as her situation. She'd been abused. "I think it's kind of apples and oranges, but I get what you're saying about not having regrets." She had plenty of them. And they were in the way of allowing someone else into her life.

"Sure, it's a bit different, but maybe not in the way you think." He leaned forward and set his elbows on the counter. "I was always kind of a loner—too smart for my own britches. Military life suited me, and the intelligence work was an even better fit."

"Wasn't it lonely?" Kelsey asked.

"I didn't think so. Not until I decided to leave. Then I began to realize just how isolated I really was. The problem was, though, by then I was too far gone. I didn't know how to open up. I got back to the real world, and I didn't have a clue. Thankfully, I met Rob Archer. He sort of insisted we become friends." He laughed again, that low, rumbly, feel-good chuckle. "Rob's a great man. I owe him a lot. Without him, I probably wouldn't have gained enough courage—or social skills—to ask your lovely grandma out."

Kelsey could feel the warmth between them, and it gave her hope. For what, she wasn't sure. She just wanted to feel that someday. "Well, that seems to be paying off for you."

"On one of my assignments, I came into contact with a lot of women who'd been abused. They had one thing in common—they didn't trust themselves anymore. Sure, they didn't have much trust in other people either, but the fundamental thing they had to learn was how to forgive themselves and accept that none of it was their fault." He frowned. "It's a tough thing."

Kelsey's throat knotted, and she knew from experience that she was a heartbeat away from an avalanche of tears. He'd drilled right into the heart of things. She only nodded.

Gram moved her hand to Kelsey's back, stroking her. "It's all right," she murmured. Then she looked to George. "You don't have to make the poor girl cry."

This made Kelsey laugh, for which she was grateful.

"I'm okay. George, you're an insightful man."

"Well, all I'll say to you—like you even want my advice, but you're getting it anyway—is that Luke is a terrific guy. I don't know the jackass who was in your life before, and I hope I never do." His eyes glinted steel. "He'd better hope that too. Anyhow, you can't do much better than Luke Westcott. His family is solid, he has a great work ethic, and he's someone I trust."

Kelsey recalled the hurt look in his eyes when she'd told him to burn his flowers. He couldn't possibly know what they meant to her. How they'd upset her. He was just trying to make amends, and for something that wasn't even his fault. So what if his ex showed up that morning? Had that really been the issue, or was it just that Kelsey didn't trust herself not to make another mistake?

She was pretty sure she knew the answer. She *had* made a mistake, but hopefully it was fixable.

She lifted her glass now in a toast of her own. "To unsolicited, awesome advice."

George clinked his glass against hers, and Gram joined in. They all took a drink.

"All righty, then," George said, rubbing his hands together, "who's hungry for some steak?"

Chapter Fourteen

LUKE GAVE UP trying to finish his dinner. His folks had invited him over, but he'd declined. He was even more upset—and bewildered—about Kelsey than he'd been earlier in the day.

Her refusal of his flowers had stung. She hadn't just declined them, she'd done the verbal equivalent of throwing them in his face. He hadn't thought Paige showing up would be that damaging to their fledgling relationship, but then he wasn't sure what to expect. Kelsey had tried to put on the brakes. She'd been honest about being hesitant. Maybe she just wasn't ready.

Which sucked, because he was. If Paige dropping in had showed him anything, it was that Kelsey was different. Special.

He set his dishes in the sink, grabbed a beer from the fridge, and went to the living room to watch football highlights. He'd just turned on *Sports Center* when headlights flashed through the window as a car pulled into the driveway.

He set his beer on the coffee table and stood up. He walked over and peered through the blinds. It was Kelsey.

Anticipation thrummed in his chest. He'd hoped she would show up. Was she here to stay, or had she come to pick up her things? He'd find out in a minute.

He went back to the couch and sat down. He sipped

his beer and tried to focus on the television. The lock on the front door clicked, and he tensed. He turned his head toward the door as she came inside.

She looked the same as earlier—her hair hanging loose and gorgeous, a light cranberry-colored jacket thrown over her long-sleeved V-neck tee and distressed jeans, and those sexy dark brown booties. Why they were sexy, he didn't know. Maybe he just felt that way about everything to do with her.

"Hey." She walked around the couch and moved into the living room.

He muted the sound on the TV. "Hey."

She dropped her purse on the chair. "Mind if I sit with you?"

He sat in the middle of the couch, rather taking up the entire thing, so he scooted to the right. "Sure. I mean, I don't mind."

Her lips curved into a weak smile. "I knew what you meant." She sat down, but on the edge of the couch. She clasped her hands together and rested them on her knees. "I wanted to explain about earlier. About the flowers."

He turned the TV off and tossed the remote onto the table. Then he angled himself toward her, bringing his knee up onto the couch. "Okay."

"First, I want to apologize. You couldn't know this, but I have a problem with flowers. As in, I hate them. Please don't ever give me a bouquet again."

There was a vehemence and darkness to her tone that set off warning bells in his head. "Got it." He wanted to ask why but sensed she was about to tell him.

She took a deep breath. The muscles in her jaw clenched. "Noah used to bring me flowers. After he hit me."

Oh, fuck. Luke's insides crumpled. He moved closer to her, but she held up her hand and shook her head. "Let me get this out."

She took a deep breath, and he heard it catch, sounding like a shudder. He ached to touch her, but kept his hands to himself.

"I haven't really told you about him. Not because I want to hide anything, but because it's…difficult. We met in college, and honestly, for me, it was love at first sight, as corny as that sounds. He wasn't abusive in the beginning." Her expression softened, and Luke could see she was recalling happier times. He tried not to feel a stab of jealousy.

She went on. "I have a lot of good memories." Her lips curved into a sad smile. "How else could I have stayed with him so long? At least, that's what I tell myself." She looked down at her lap. "It takes the sting from my shame."

Emotion rushed through him—anger, frustration, concern, and anguish. He gently touched her chin and tipped her head up. "Hey, there's no need to feel ashamed. I'm sure I have a lot to learn about abuse, but what I do know is that it wasn't your fault. Not even staying with him for however long you did." He cupped the side of her face.

She nuzzled her cheek against him. "Thank you. You're right, and my brain knows that, but my heart, my soul…sometimes they forget."

"I'm glad you told me a little about him." He wanted to know more but was also a bit afraid. Luke already hated this man for everything he did know, for the pain he'd caused Kelsey. "And I will listen to whatever you want to share—now or in the future."

Her gaze glowed with appreciation. "I don't talk about him much. It's not just that I don't like to think of him—which I don't—or the shame factor. It's also the headspace. I spent a long time trying to dissect how I'd been so stupid and how I could've done things differently." Her eyes darkened before she tipped her head down. "I wondered why I let him do that to me, why I didn't retaliate. I thought of all the ways I should've hurt him in return."

He grew agitated listening to the agony in her tone. He started thinking of all the ways he'd like to hurt the bastard. "It's normal to want that. *I* want that. Well, not for you to hurt him," he clarified. "Honestly, I'd like a shot at him. A man that would hit a woman deserves to suffer."

Her head came up, her eyes wide. "He *is* suffering, I hope. Anyway, it doesn't matter. He doesn't deserve to take up any part of my life. I gave him far too much."

He saw the grit and determination in her gaze, in the tense set of her mouth. "I have such immense respect for you," he said softly. "To think that you've worked through this and come out stronger on the other side."

She let out a light laugh and straightened, causing him to drop his hand from her face. "I'm working on it. I still have issues. As you saw earlier."

"We all have issues, don't we?"

"I guess. What are yours? Just reappearing exes?"

His issues. Yeah, those. "Reappearing exes whose hearts I've broken, apparently." He stretched his folded leg out and put both feet on the floor.

It was her turn to bend her knee and turn toward him, resting her elbow on the back of the couch. "You didn't realize that?"

"Not to the level that she said this morning." He sent

her a wry glance. "She's still hung up on me."

"I could see that."

He smiled at the irony in her tone. "I admit I was a bit blind to…things. It took me a while to realize she was more into the relationship than I was. Moving back here gave me the distance I needed to break things off. Shit, that sounds so cowardly." He turned his head to look at her. "In my defense, I didn't see it. Like I said, I was a blind asshole."

"I don't think you meant to be an asshole. Or to hurt her. That's not the Luke I've come to know." She stared at him a moment. "Unless you've been hiding who you really are, in which case I'd have to leave. I can't do that again. I need to know who I'm with."

That socked him right in the gut. She'd been with someone who'd had some whole other side to him. He owed her the truth. Right now.

He turned toward her again, mirroring her position, complete with his elbow on the back of the couch. "I care about you a lot, Kelsey. More than I've cared for anyone. That said, I'm maybe a bit more than an introvert. Some might even call me a loner. I like my space. I honestly don't know how good I'll be at a long-term, serious relationship. Paige was the first one I'd tried, and it didn't go well. There's nothing I'd hate more than hurting you."

Her gaze was guarded. "What are you saying? Do you want to stop seeing each other?"

Hell, he was botching this. He took her hands in his. "No, definitely not. I just wanted you to know about my…issues."

Her eyes widened briefly, and her brows arched. "Oh, right. Issues. I did ask."

"Yes, but I was going to tell you anyway. You

deserve total honesty."

A soft smile fluttered across her mouth. "Thank you. This morning when you introduced me to Paige, you called me your girlfriend. Is that true?"

He hadn't given it any thought when he'd said it—the word had just come out. But it fit. "For me, yes. But you can tell me otherwise."

She shook her head. "No. I think I'd like to be your girlfriend."

Joy bubbled in his chest, and he smiled because he couldn't *not* smile. He leaned forward and kissed her, a light touching of their lips. "Consider it done."

She twined her arms around his neck and opened her mouth against his, kissing him with heat and fervor. He clasped her sides and massaged her through her jacket, then brought his hands around to push it from her shoulders.

She shrugged out of it and let it drop to the floor. Without breaking the kiss, she knelt up, rising over him. Her tongue plunged down into his mouth, teasing him. Every part of him ached for her.

Her fingers delved into his hair, her nails raking his scalp. She straddled him, her knees spearing into the couch on either side of his hips. He grasped her waist and pulled her down while he arched up. They both wore jeans, and they were too damn cumbersome to allow what he sought. He wanted her hot sheath bare and ready for him.

She moaned into his mouth as she ground against him. He dug his hands into her ass, desperate for more. She ran her hands down his back and grabbed the hem of his T-shirt. Her fingers grazed his bare flesh as she drew it upward. They pulled apart long enough for her to tug it over his head and throw it over the back of the couch.

They renewed the kiss, their mouths open and hungry. She gripped his shoulders as she plundered his mouth. Then her hands skimmed over his collarbones and down his chest, her thumbs flicking his nipples as they moved south.

Desire beat through him, taking him to new heights of arousal. This was more than sex. This was a connection he'd never felt.

She tore her mouth from his and kissed along his throat, pushing him back against the couch as she descended. Her lips and tongue trailed along his flesh. Again, she stopped at his nipples, teasing them briefly before she continued toward his waistband.

Her hands made quick work of his button and zipper, undoing his jeans with effortless precision. His cock was hard and ready, so eager for her touch.

She tugged at his jeans, working them down over his hips. He came up off the couch to help her, and she soon stripped them away from his quivering body. He watched as she settled herself between his legs and inched his boxer briefs lower, slowly exposing his aching cock.

She looked up at him, her tongue darting over her lips as she gave him a wicked little grin. He snagged his fingers in her hair and moaned her name.

Without bothering to pull his underwear completely off, she put her lips on him. Her wet heat surrounded the tip and then her mouth descended as her tongue stroked his length. He tried to hold himself in check but couldn't. He thrust up into her, and she took him to the back of her throat. He felt her swallow, and the contraction sent blood screaming to his balls. This was not going to last long.

She seemed to realize this as she eased back and used her hand to work his shaft for several strokes. He squeezed his eyes shut as pleasure cascaded through him. God, the ecstasy was almost unbearable.

She took him deeper again, sucking hard. Lights danced behind his eyes. "Kelsey, I'm not going to—" His orgasm built, but she pulled way with an audible smack. He heard her breathing, hard and fast, and just barely managed to hold on.

"Should we move to the bedroom?" Her voice was dark and husky and so damn seductive, he couldn't stand it.

He sat up and pulled her to straddle his lap. "I don't care where we go. I just want you. Now."

She pulled her shirt off and unfastened her bra, letting it fall between them. "So take me."

With a grunt, he cupped the underside of her breast and pushed it up as he lowered his mouth to devour her nipple. She thrust her hands into his hair once more, tugging at the strands, but he was heedless of any pain—just a persistent, thrumming lust that only she could satisfy.

But it was more than lust. So much more. He couldn't wait to come with her, but at the same time didn't want it to ever end.

He wrapped his arms around her waist and stood.

She sucked in a breath. "Whoa. *Luke*." She wrapped her legs around him as he carried her to the bedroom. He lifted his mouth from her breast and claimed her lips. Their tongues met in a deep kiss that seemed to speak all the words he couldn't form just now.

In the bedroom, he stood her at the end of the bed, then undid her jeans. Gently, he pushed them down over her hips, along with her underwear. She sat on the edge of the bed, and he knelt to take off her boots so he could get her completely naked. Realizing he wasn't completely naked, he stripped his underwear off then pushed her legs apart and knelt between them.

She opened her eyes and there was a silent, still moment where they just looked at each other, their bodies barely touching. He stared into her pale-blue irises and gently touched her inner thigh, dragging his knuckles along her soft flesh. Her eyes narrowed infinitesimally, and her lips parted.

He worked his hand higher until he grazed her cleft. She opened her legs a little more, and he used his thumb on her clit, stroking and pushing then tweaking it between his fingers. Little pants escaped her mouth, spurring his need ever higher.

Keeping his gaze locked with hers, he slipped his finger into her. She wilted a little and clasped his shoulders. He slid in as far as he could go, then withdrew. Her fingertips dug into his flesh. This time, he put two fingers into her, thrusting slowly. She gasped, and her eyes finally closed. "*Luke.*"

He wrapped his other hand around her neck. "Open your eyes. Look at me when you come."

He withdrew his hands until she acquiesced. Her eyes came open, and in their depths, he saw pleasure and awe and something he couldn't define. He imagined he looked the same. At least, that was how he felt.

"Tell me when you're close," he rasped. He pumped into her faster now, his thumb flicking her clit. He brought his face closer as he held her nape tight in his grip.

Her breathing came faster as her hips moved with his hand. "Yes. More."

He quickened his pace, driving into her as her

impassioned cries filled the room.

"I'm close. So close." Her eyelids fluttered. "I can't."

"Look at me." He cupped her neck and brought his lips almost to hers. He could feel her breath.

Her muscles contracted around his fingers as she cried out. He claimed her mouth as he took her cries into himself, kissing her deep and hard.

After she quieted and her body subsided, he withdrew from her, going to his nightstand to grab a condom. When he returned, she took it from him and stood up from the bed. "My turn," she said, her gaze dark and commanding.

He arched a brow. "What do you want?"

"You. On your back." She pivoted and lightly pushed against his chest.

He fell back as he watched her. She was lean and beautiful, her nipples dark pink peaks atop lush, silken globes. Her waist tapered to slightly flared hips, and her long legs beckoned him to bury himself between them.

She came around to the side of the bed and leaned one knee down as she bent to slip the condom along his shaft. Her touch sent him to the stratosphere, reminding him of how close he'd been in the living room. Then she threw her leg over him and positioned herself above his hips. She gripped his cock and brought it between her thighs.

Slowly, she came down, her sheath taking him in. He tried to hold back, to let her take charge, but he just wanted to grip her hips and drive into her. Forcing himself to lie back, he directed his attention to her breasts. They swayed above him, tantalizing and gorgeous. He reached up and cupped them, his fingers tweaking and pulling on the nipples while he massaged the soft flesh.

She took him inside her to the hilt, her hips grinding against his. Her inner thighs hugged his hips as she rocked against him, slowly at first, teasing him. Buried in her wet heat, her muscles clenching around him, Luke fought to keep a handle on himself. But then she began to move faster. He didn't want it to be over. Not yet.

He rose off the bed and snaked his hand around the nape of her neck, drawing her down so he could kiss her. She held him by the shoulders and angled her head to kiss him, her tongue plunging deep into his mouth. After a moment, she broke free, gasping as her hips worked over him. He took her nipple between his teeth, tugging the flesh before soothing it with his lips and tongue.

She pushed him down, her palm flat on his chest as she rode him faster. She arched up and ground down, her hips snapping against his. He tried to hang on, but he was too far gone. Pleasure rushed through him and plunged him headfirst over the edge into pure ecstasy as his orgasm tore through him. He yelled and bucked and barely thought to touch her, putting his fingers against her clit and coaxing her orgasm forth.

She bored down on him so hard that it was like coming a second time. White lights danced behind his eyes as he rode the wave of bliss.

A moment later, she bent over him, her breasts grazing his chest. He wrapped his arms around her and held her close as he pressed his lips to her temple, then her cheek. She turned her head and kissed him, her lips moving gently over his. Her breath, soft and sexy, mingled with his, and he could only think that he never wanted this moment to end.

He brushed her long hair back from her face and

cupped her head, kissing her as he rolled to his side. He stroked her cheekbone, her jaw, and she sighed into his mouth.

Reluctantly, he left her. "Be right back," he whispered.

After disposing of the condom and cleaning up, he came back to the bed. She'd crawled under the bedcovers, her body curled up and her hair tossed carelessly over the pillow. He climbed in behind her and gathered her close.

She sighed again and pressed a kiss to the back of his wrist. "Good night."

Contentment filled his soul. "Good night."

Chapter Fifteen
♥♪

KELSEY PRACTICALLY FLOATED into the library on Thursday. Being Luke's girlfriend was amazing. He was kind, considerate, sexy as hell, and even cooked. She'd gone back to her apartment to pick things up a couple of times, but had now spent a week living with Luke.

Living with him? They hadn't discussed the situation long-term, but yeah, for now, they were living together.

Part of her said they needed to have that conversation, that it was important to make sure they were both on the same page. But another part of her said to shut up and just enjoy what was happening in the moment. For now, she was listening to that part. As well as to her therapist, whom she'd finally seen a few days ago. She'd been supportive of Kelsey's take-it-slow approach with Luke and had helped her work through some of her lingering fear.

As Kelsey opened up the library, her assistant, Marci, arrived. Marci was a grad student at nearby Williver College, studying education. She planned to teach elementary school. "Morning, Kelsey! What's going on today?"

"The usual," Kelsey said. "Can you handle story time today? I have a few things I'd like to work on upstairs."

Marci nodded as she locked her purse in a cabinet behind the counter. "Sure thing. How are plans coming for the Halloween event?"

Earlier in the week, Kelsey and Luke had come up

with an idea to host a library event at West Arch Estate next weekend. Luke and his partners would open the pumpkin patch, offer hayrides, and, of course, pour wine for the adults. Meanwhile, Kelsey would host a cookie-decorating area and story time with a craft. She and Marci had brainstormed what to do on Tuesday.

"Good. Barley and Bran said they'd donate the cookies for the decorating. We just need to get the decorating supplies."

Marci flipped her shoulder-length brown hair over her shoulder. "Sounds great. I hit the craft store yesterday and picked up a bunch of stuff. Today I was planning to print off coloring sheets."

Kelsey grinned. "We will be more than ready come next Saturday. Would you shelve books while I check my e-mail?"

"Sure thing." Marci took off while Kelsey sat at the desk to the left of the counter and pulled up her e-mail. She scanned it quickly and saw a message from Darryl Gray, the historian.

Kelsey's pulse sped as she read. He'd found some information about Bird's Nest Ranch. They were still waiting for the results from the testing the archaeologist had done in the hope of finding out when the house had burned down. But Darryl's findings had nothing to do with the fire.

She reread what he'd written: "I've found evidence from 1894 that the Bird's Nest Ranch was a brothel."

Marci appeared at the desk. "Everything all right?"

Kelsey realized she'd gasped and that she was staring, wide-eyed, at the monitor. She shook her head to clear away the surprise. "Yes. It's fine." She pulled out her phone and texted the others—Crystal, Brooke, and Alaina—to tell them the news.

Their responses were almost immediate. To a person, they were shocked and dismayed.

Crystal asked if Dorinda still owned the ranch at that time. Kelsey couldn't tell from Darryl's e-mail, so she dashed off a response asking for more information.

He got back to her within a few minutes saying that he didn't know. He'd found a newspaper article with a line mentioning the "Bird's Nest Brothel above Ribbon Ridge." He said he would continue to research it because his interest was piqued. He'd no idea there'd been a bordello in the area.

Kelsey sent the information to her friends along with her disappointment at learning that Dorinda's homestead had become a house of ill repute. Everyone shared her chagrin and looked forward to finding the truth. Crystal was particularly passionate, texting that she was more committed than ever to finding out Dorinda's story. They all wanted to know if she'd somehow been driven to open a brothel or if something else had happened to oust her from the home she'd built.

Kelsey set her phone aside to respond to a few other e-mails. A few minutes later, it rang. She expected it to be one of the girls, so she didn't look at the screen before picking it up and saying hello.

"Kelsey?" The feminine voice was a bit familiar, but it wasn't Brooke or Crystal or Alaina.

"Yes? Who is this?"

"It's Lisa Putnam."

Shit. Noah's mother. Kelsey's stomach dropped to the floor, and her mouth went dry. "Um, hi."

"I know you must be surprised to hear from me. How are you?"

Kelsey had always liked Lisa. She'd often wondered if

she'd been aware of her son's violent nature, but nothing the woman had ever said or done had led Kelsey to think that she was. That made Kelsey ponder whether Lisa had been abused by Noah's father. But they'd divorced when Noah was twelve, and he'd simply vanished from Noah's life. In retrospect, that should've been a huge red flag.

"I'm fine." Kelsey didn't ask how Lisa was. She didn't care. She didn't want these people—Noah's family—in her life.

"I'm so glad to hear it. I'm sure you know that Noah got out of jail."

"Yes." *And I already have a restraining order.* The judge had granted it for a period of one year. It had been easy to get, and renewing it wouldn't be difficult.

"He's staying with me. I wanted you to know how sorry he is. He's in counseling and doing really well. I just thought you'd want to know."

Actually, she didn't. Anxiety tripped through her, and she began to shake. "Lisa, I've moved on with my life." She couldn't even bring herself to say she was glad he was doing well. She didn't want to feel anything where it came to him—good, bad, ugly. She'd worked damn hard to push him out of her life, and she needed him to stay there.

"I understand," Lisa said quietly. "I'm sorry to have bothered you."

"Thank you, and please—" Kelsey swallowed her apprehension and summoned the steel she'd strived to hone. "Please don't call me again. Good-bye." She hung up without waiting for a response, then went into the settings on her phone to block Lisa's number. In fact, she'd blocked Lisa ages ago. It must've been a new number.

Kelsey stood and went to open the box of books, which patrons had ordered from other libraries. As she busied herself with shelving them in the pickup area, her adrenaline settled and she began to relax. She forced herself to think of something other than Noah. Dorinda and the ranch. Rather, the brothel. Ugh. Okay, not that.

Luke, duh. Luke would cheer her up. Just conjuring his handsome face with his super-sexy stare made her smile. Much better. She finished the shelving and planned to go upstairs to work on the exhibit for a bit. Story time was in full swing, and Marci had it handled.

As if he'd been summoned right out of her brain, Luke walked into the library at that moment. Kelsey's heart tripped as she caught sight of him. He wore dark jeans, his scuffed work boots, and a plaid shirt with the sleeves rolled up to his elbows over a blue T-shirt. He scanned the interior before his gaze landed on her. His eyes lit, and his lips curved into a smile.

She met him in front of the checkout counter. "You finally made it in."

"Technically, I came in the other day, but I think we've agreed to forget about that."

Because that was when he'd brought the stupid flowers. She winced. "Sorry. Well, I'm glad you're here now. Do you want a tour?"

"Of course." He arched a sexy brow at her. "I hope it includes your office."

She laughed. "I don't have an office. There's a conference room and kitchen upstairs. Will that do?"

"I don't know. Let me check it out." He raked her from head to toe with a provocative stare that made her shiver.

"Come on, I'll show you around before you

thoroughly distract me." She linked her arm through his and took him on a tour of the downstairs. When she was finished, she led him toward the stairs. "I'll take you up to show you the Ribbon Ridge exhibit space." She gave him a sidelong look. "*Not* the conference room."

He huffed out a breath and donned a look of mock disappointment. At least she thought it was a put-on. Maybe it wasn't.

"You've put together an impressive library," he said as they climbed the stairs.

"I owe it to the Archers and their generosity. It wouldn't have been possible without their grant."

He chuckled. "They can afford it."

"Sure, but not everyone who can would give back the way that they do."

"Very true. And they do it because they want to, not for the tax breaks."

They reached the exhibit space, and she showed him around everything she'd set up.

"Also impressive," he said. "I keep forgetting to ask if you've had any news from the archaeologist. Do I need to worry they're going to classify my vineyard as some valuable historic site?"

She shook her head. "You were there. She said she didn't think that would happen. But no, we haven't heard anything. We did learn today that the ranch became a brothel at one point."

He turned to look at her. "A what?"

"A brothel."

His brows climbed his forehead. "Whoa. That gives our property some unintended character."

"The historical society is doing more research," she said. "We'd love to know how that came about."

"Yeah, me too. Let me know when you find out." He snaked his arms around her waist and pulled her close. "In the meantime, I have something for you."

She saw the mischievous glint in his eye and was instantly curious. "You do? Does this involve the conference room?"

He laughed. "It *could*. But no." He reached into his pocket and pulled something out. Then he took her hand, and her breath caught. What was he *doing*?

When he didn't drop to one knee, she relaxed slightly. He clasped something around her wrist. She held up her wrist and saw the filigreed book charm. She gasped, then smiled. "It's the bracelet from Oktoberfest! How did you do that?"

He grinned. "I might've taken the vendor's card that night when your back was turned. And I might've called her to buy it."

Kelsey turned her wrist this way and that. "I love it." She rested her hand on his shoulder and looked into his eyes. "Thank you." It was perhaps the most thoughtful gift she'd ever received.

She moved closer until their chests were touching, stood on her toes, and kissed him. He swept her up against him, and when the kiss was over, she was breathless.

"I suppose I should let you get back to work." His tone echoed with regret.

Suddenly, the conference room idea had extreme merit. She grasped the edges of his shirt over his chest. "So you wanna see the conference room?"

His eyes glinted with desire. "I thought you'd never ask. Really. And I was *so* disappointed."

She waggled her brows at him before taking his hand and leading him into the conference room. Once they were inside, she closed the door. "Um, there's no lock."

"Does your assistant come up here?"

"Just to take a break, but she's busy with story time and will be for at least"—she glanced at the clock on the microwave on the counter—"another fifteen minutes."

"Then we'd better get busy." He reached out and took her hand, pulling her against him. He framed her face with his hands and kissed her long and deep.

Kelsey melted into him, all the while thinking this wasn't her best idea but unable to put a stop to it. Except... She pulled back. "Do you have a condom?"

His lips spread in a sexy, arrogant grin that did crazy things to her insides. "In my wallet." He pulled it from his back pocket, withdrew the aforementioned item, and tossed the wallet on the table. He turned his attention back to her and held up the wrapped square.

She snatched it from his fingertips and reached for his waistband, popping his button open. She thrust her hand lower and cupped his rigid length. "Mmm, you're quite ready."

He growled out her name before tugging her against him and kissing her. He speared his tongue into her mouth as he thrust his hips into her hand. She rubbed her hand along his heat while desire pooled in her core.

He pivoted with her and set her on the edge of the table. "You wore a skirt today. How fortuitous." He slid his palms up her thighs, squeezing her flesh, until he found the waistband of her underwear. She lifted herself off the table as he worked them down and pulled them off.

She undid his jeans all the way and coaxed his cock from his briefs. Using her teeth, she tore open the condom wrapper.

So Right

"God, I love it when you do that. So sexy," he said, swirling his thumb over her clit.

Pleasure pulsed through her. Whenever he stroked her there, it seemed an orgasm was never far away. He already knew her body so well. She thrilled to his touch.

She rolled the condom over him and cupped his balls. He groaned and leaned in to kiss her. He clasped her hips and brought her to the edge of the table, meeting her there, his cock nudging her opening.

She opened her thighs wider and clasped the base of his shaft, guiding him into her. He thrust inside, burying himself to the root, and she wrapped her legs around his waist.

Everything else was a blur of movement and pleasure as he stroked into her with fast, hard snaps. She wanted to cry out but couldn't. She clutched the back of his neck and kissed him harder as her orgasm slammed into her.

He came right after, groaning into her mouth. She held him close as reality came back to her.

He withdrew, and she pointed him to the doorway that led to a bathroom. She found her underwear and set herself to rights. A moment later, he came out, his lips curved into a satisfied smile she was sure he'd wear all day.

"You've thoroughly corrupted me," she said.

He walked to her and kissed her cheek. "Guilty. Without regret, by the way."

She let out a laugh. "Come on, I need to get back downstairs."

He walked down with her, and she saw him out. "Feel free to drop by anytime."

He winked at her. "I will accept that invitation."

She held up her wrist. "Thank you for the bracelet. I

love it."

He stared at her a moment, and she had the sense he was going to say something. Instead, he kissed her softly. "See you later."

She closed the door and watched him walk away, happiness swelling in her heart.

AFTER SPENDING HIS Monday morning outside in the vineyard, Luke walked into the winery to grab lunch. He headed to the kitchen and was surprised to see both of his brothers and Hayden there. "Guess we're all on the same schedule today."

Cam smiled at him. "Guess so. We're heating up Mom's leftover stew."

Luke opened the cupboard to grab a glass and froze for a second. He and Kelsey had eaten dinner at his parents' last night. They'd had stew. Which meant Mom had dropped this off this morning.

He turned from the cupboard and exhaled. "What did she tell you?" He waited for the barrage of questions, or, perhaps more accurately, the ration of shit.

Cam's smile broadened to a grin. "She *really* likes Kelsey."

This wasn't news to Luke. She'd been thrilled when, after inviting him to dinner last night, he'd asked if he could bring along his girlfriend. That single word had sent her into paroxysms of delight.

Not that Luke had any problem with that. He was

pretty giddy himself. In fact, he was counting the minutes until Kelsey got here. They were going to spend the afternoon finalizing details about the Halloween event they were hosting this Saturday.

"So what's the scoop?" Hayden asked, stirring the stew, which they were reheating on the stove top.

Luke poured himself some iced tea from the fridge. "There's no 'scoop.' We're dating. What's the big deal?"

"Good question," Hayden said. "It's not like when Cam got serious about Brooke. That was a *massive* deal." He shot a teasing grin toward his best friend, which earned him an eye roll from Cam.

Jamie leaned against the counter near the door. He was drinking a glass of what looked like apple cider.

Luke inclined his head toward the glass. "Is that the cider for this Saturday?"

Jamie glanced toward Hayden and Cam. "See how he tries to deflect?"

Luke shook his head, then leaned back against the counter next to the fridge. "Clearly you all want details. Ask away."

"Are you guys living together?" Jamie asked. "My running route takes me by the house, and I notice her car is still there."

"Wow, sounds serious," Hayden said.

Damn, they had to open with a tough one? He and Kelsey hadn't discussed the living arrangements long-term. They were just happy being together. "She's still staying with me, yes. Her apartment, as I've pointed out, is crap."

"Is she still looking for a place?" Jamie persisted.

"Yes." Maybe. Probably not. Luke made a mental note to ask and to also reiterate that she was welcome to stay as long as she liked. Which, he supposed, suggested they were living together—at least in his mind. It wasn't as if anyone was sleeping on the futon.

"Well, I'm thrilled for you," Cam said. "I hope this works out better than Paige. Speaking of her, I heard through the grapevine"—he winced—"sorry, pun not intended. I heard she interviewed at Bellwether last week."

"Yeah." Luke hadn't heard from her since she'd shown up at his house. "Do you know if she got the job?"

Cam shook his head. "I don't think so. I think they offered it to someone from the area. Can't imagine the prospect of her living nearby made you too excited."

No, but then it also hadn't made him upset. "It doesn't affect me. She's in the past."

Hayden stirred the stew again. "Clearly, since you're all hot and heavy with Kelsey. Which is cool. I like her a lot. This Halloween event is going to be great."

"I think so too." Luke wasn't looking for their approval, but it was nice to have. Especially since he liked Kelsey more than a lot.

In fact, he was pretty sure he was falling in love with her. He thought about her constantly and could hardly wait to be with her when they were apart. And when they were together, he never wanted their time to end. Living with her—yep, he'd call it that, at least to himself—felt so comfortable. She didn't care that he might want to tune out and watch *Sports Center* or work outside in the yard. She was as busy as he was, doing library stuff or reading a book. They shared this companionable silence that he'd never experienced before.

"Stew's ready," Hayden said. He looked over at

Luke. "You joining us?"

"Sure. Kelsey will be here in about a half hour so we can walk through what's left to arrange for Saturday."

Cam grabbed bowls from the cupboard. "You sound really happy. I'm glad."

Luke turned and set his glass down on the counter so he could pull spoons from the drawer. "She's pretty special."

Yeah, things were serious. He hoped she felt the same way.

Chapter Sixteen
☙

SATURDAY MORNING DAWNED cool and cloudy, much to Kelsey's chagrin. She crossed her fingers that the weather forecast was accurate and that it would burn off by late morning. She was just glad it wasn't raining.

She and Luke were the first to arrive at the winery at seven o'clock, but were soon joined by Marci and the West Arch crew. By the time they opened at nine, everything was ready to go. Business was relatively slow until shortly after ten, right when the sun started to peek through the clouds.

Kelsey was manning the cookie-decorating station when Alaina and Evan arrived with their toddler daughter, Alexa. Alaina gave Kelsey a big hug. "What a fantastic event! This is classic Ribbon Ridge."

Evan looked at his wife. "Don't forget to tell her about the e-mail Crystal got. You wanted me to remind you." He helped Alexa into a chair at the table.

Alaina nodded as she smiled at him. "I did, thank you." She turned to Kelsey, who was presenting Alexa with a cookie in the shape of a pumpkin. "Crystal heard from the archaeologist."

Kelsey straightened. "Do tell!"

"They dated the fire to 1901. Ish. It's hard to be super accurate, but that's their best guess based on the testing."

"I wonder if it was still a brothel at that time," Kelsey said.

"Crystal said the same thing. She's in LA right now, but she's looking forward to doing more research." Alaina chuckled. "I think she's going to move into the historical society until she's figured out what happened to Dorinda."

"She seems very interested in her," Kelsey said.

"If by interested, you mean obsessed, then yes. Especially since we heard about the brothel. She's desperate to know if Dorinda was part of that or if she'd moved on by then." Alaina helped her daughter frost the pumpkin cookie. "People and stories interest Crystal—she's a natural-born storyteller. I keep trying to convince her to write a script."

"About Dorinda?"

"About something. I know she wants to—she just has to set aside her self-defeating attitude." Alaina set the frosted cookie on a napkin in front of Alexa. "Do you want some sprinkles?"

"Sprinkles!" Alexa reached for a container of Halloween-shaped decorative sprinkles to shake over her cookie.

"Well, I hope she does that," Kelsey said, thinking that the pursuit of one's dreams was vitally important to finding happiness.

She glanced over to the hayride stop where a few families were lined up, waiting for Luke to return on the tractor. Emotion gathered in her chest as she anticipated seeing him again. Emotion she somewhat recognized.

Was she in love with him? Just thinking the L word made her tremble. She'd felt so betrayed by that emotion. She wasn't sure she was ready to let it in again.

Shaking her head, she focused on the kids at the

table. After a quick lunch, she read Halloween stories to the kids and handed out lollipops. Gram and George stopped by, holding hands. Kelsey didn't think Gram had ever looked happier.

George excused himself to go check out Luke's tractor while another load of families was climbing into the hay-stacked trailer he was pulling. Gram sighed as she watched him walk away.

She touched Gram's arm. "You and George are really happy."

Gram turned, smiling. "Yes. Frighteningly so." She laughed. "When I came to Ribbon Ridge to blow off steam for a bit, I never imagined I'd stay. Let alone take a job. Or fall in love."

There was that L word again. "Have you? Fallen in love?"

Gram nodded. "I think so. I'm quite out of practice, of course. I fell in love with your grandpa a lifetime ago. But I suppose it's like riding a bike."

Kelsey wasn't sure she agreed. Riding a bike was a repeatable endeavor—one you could learn and practice and improve upon. After Noah, she'd accepted that she just sucked at falling in love and really had no interest in trying it again. But now... It was hard to compare what was happening with Luke to what she'd felt for Noah. With Noah, she'd known, almost immediately. Luke was different. She felt a quiet peace with him that she didn't necessarily equate with the tumult of falling in love. At least in her experience.

No, she couldn't relate it to riding a bike.

"So what are your plans, then?" Kelsey asked. "Will you just stay at the Archers' apartment for now?"

"Actually, George has asked me to move in with him, and I'm considering it." Gram laughed and waved her hand. "Oh, who am I kidding? I'll probably tell him yes tonight. We have a romantic dinner planned."

Kelsey wrapped her in a fierce hug. "I'm so glad you'll be staying here."

Gram hugged her back. "Me too, dear." When they broke apart, Gram studied her intently. "What about you and Luke? Are you moving in with him?"

They'd discussed it briefly this week. Actually, Luke had brought it up, and Kelsey had neatly changed the subject. File that right along with keeping love at bay. "Not right now."

The light in Gram's eye faded. "Is something wrong?"

"No, not at all. Everything's great. I'm just taking things very slowly."

Gram patted her shoulder. "As you should, dear. I'm sorry if I'm being insensitive. You two just seem to be getting on very well. I like seeing you happy as much as you like seeing me that way."

Of course she did. She leaned over and kissed Gram's cheek. "Thank you."

George came back and said he'd agreed to take over driving the tractor so that Luke could have a much-deserved break. Hearing that, Kelsey asked if Gram would mind watching the cookie table so she could grab something for Luke to eat. Gram was eager to help, and so Kelsey took off into the winery to fetch a sandwich and a Coke for Luke. She grabbed a Diet Coke for herself and juggled everything as she hurried back outside.

The afternoon had turned bright and warm. She blinked against the sun and contemplated going back inside for her sunglasses.

Then Luke came toward her, his handsome face

creased in a smile as his gaze dipped to the sandwich in her hands. "You brought me lunch." He dropped a lingering kiss on her mouth.

The anticipation she'd felt earlier curled into an irrepressible joy. "Yes. Do you want to sit?"

"Nah, I'm good. Been sitting in the tractor most of the day." He took the sandwich and led her to a table near the winery, where they had extra arts supplies stocked and ready if they needed them. Marci was doing a great job with the craft table.

She opened his Coke and set it on the table, then opened her can. "This has exceeded my expectations." She looked around at the families enjoying the beautiful fall day and just felt happy to be a part of it.

"Mine too."

The soft, sultry sound of his voice drew her to look at him. He was staring at her as if he'd been referring to *her* instead of the event.

"Are you being a dork?"

"Probably. You make me act all dorky." He made a silly face before taking a bite of sandwich.

She chuckled before sipping her Diet Coke.

After he swallowed, he took a drink. "Cam asked if we wanted to join him and Brooke tonight for dinner at The Arch and Vine. We all agreed we'd be too exhausted to cook." Cam and Brooke were, of course, busy pouring wine today and hopefully expanding their club membership as well as selling cases and cases of their latest vintage.

"Sure, sounds good."

"Kelsey!" Gram waved from the cookie table. "I need more sprinkles."

"Oops, I better go." Kelsey turned, but Luke shot his arm around her waist and pulled her against him.

"Can I have a kiss first?" Something about the way he'd physically stopped her from leaving rankled her.

"We're in the middle of everything."

"Not really, we're off to the side." He let go of her, his eyes clouding. "Sorry. Did I do something wrong?"

No. He'd just reminded her of Noah, who'd been fond of asking her to bestow kisses on him at all sorts of odd times, like in the middle of the grocery store or while they were waiting in line at the movie theater. But she wouldn't make the same mistake she'd made with the flowers. Luke hadn't intended anything other than doing what boyfriends did with their girlfriends.

She stood on her toes and kissed his cheek. "No. We're good."

As she made her way back to the cookie table, she couldn't shake the feeling that all this happiness she'd been feeling would disappear, that she was doomed to crash and burn. That was the outcome she was familiar with. Happily ever after, it seemed, was for other people.

ॐ

IT HAD BEEN an exhausting day, but Luke couldn't think of any place he'd rather be than laughing over dinner with Kelsey, his brother, and his brother's fiancée. They'd already decided to make today's event an annual thing, which in Luke's mind bound him to Kelsey, assuming she was still Ribbon Ridge's librarian.

Luke reached over and took Kelsey's hand beneath the table. She clasped her fingers around his but didn't look at him since she was chatting with Brooke. The book charm from her bracelet fell against his hand.

She'd worn it every day since he'd given it to her. He smiled.

Cam finished his beer and picked up the pitcher to fill his glass to the halfway mark. "Another beer?" he asked Luke.

"Sure." Luke pushed his glass toward his brother across the table. "About the same."

"You working tomorrow?" Cam asked.

"I don't know. Maybe."

"Dude, you deserve a day off. Hell, you deserve a vacation."

And he'd take one in January or February like he usually did. The question was whether he'd go alone. He recalled the conversation he'd had with Kelsey weeks ago, when he'd sort of invited her to go away with him. What had once seemed a distant possibility was now something he wanted desperately. She'd never been off the West Coast. He began to think of all the places he could take her and wondered if she even had a passport. Would she be able to take time off from the library? Hell, maybe she could just close it for a week. People could go without borrowing books and movies for a week, couldn't they?

He looked over at Kelsey. Going without her wasn't an option. Apparently, the loner didn't want to be alone anymore. He wanted to be with her. Even tomorrow loomed large and boring since she'd be at the library all afternoon.

What the hell had happened to him? He normally had no problem facing a day by himself. In fact, he relished it.

He shook the thoughts away and dragged himself back to what Cam had said. "You know me, I'm a workaholic."

"Always have been, even in school. You and Jamie were pulling straight As and my not-too-shabby three-point-seven-five looked like crap."

Kelsey looked over at Cam as she picked up her pint of cider. "That's nothing to sneeze at."

"Said the girl who graduated a year early," Luke said.

Brooke leaned forward. "Is that true?"

Kelsey swallowed her cider and set the glass back on the table. "Yes." She sent Luke a teasing smile. "Thanks for outing me."

He blinked and teased her back. "Is it a secret?"

"Maybe. Now you have to share a secret."

"Oh, man. I don't know." He tried to think of something she wouldn't know. They'd shared so much over the past couple of weeks.

Cam snorted. "This is easy. One of the many things this overachiever did in high school was work on the newspaper. He wrote a regular sports column, but what people didn't know was that he was also the advice columnist, Dear Granny."

Oh hell. Luke hadn't thought of that in years.

Kelsey let go of his hand and turned toward him in the booth. Her eyes sparkled with mirth. "Seriously? I'm trying to imagine." She looked over at Cam. "Any chance your folks have a newspaper or two lying around?"

Cam laughed. "I'm sure. Just ask my mom next time you see her. She'd be delighted to share all sorts of things."

"It's true," Brooke said. "She's shown me every embarrassing picture of Cam, including him running around naked at age four with his underwear on his head."

Cam dropped his head and shook it before shooting

her a wide grin. "You had to mention that."

Brooke shrugged. "Seems only fair since you spilled your brother's secret."

"That means I should spill one for you. Let's see—"

Brooke put her fingers in front of his mouth. "I have no idea what you were going to say, but shut up." She turned to Kelsey and Luke. "I had to go to my prom with green hair. Do *not* color your hair at home for the first time on prom day."

"Yikes!" Kelsey covered her mouth and giggled.

Brooke grinned. "But really, I want to hear more about Dear Granny. What sort of questions did you get?"

Luke opened his mouth to respond, but someone approached the table—a guy with dark hair and an extremely nervous look in his eye.

"Kelsey?"

She turned her head, but not before Luke caught the spark of fear in her gaze. "Noah. What are you doing here?"

Adrenaline pumped through Luke. It took everything he had not to jump up from the bench and launch himself over the table at her ex. "This is Noah?"

Noah's gaze flicked toward him, but only briefly before returning to Kelsey. "Can we go somewhere to talk? Just for a few minutes."

She was quiet for a moment, and Luke was afraid she was considering it. Why would she do that? He wanted to beat the guy into the ground.

"I don't have anything to say to you," she finally said, her voice quivering.

Luke's heart twisted. He clenched his hands into tight fists as anger roiled inside him.

Noah nodded once. "That's okay. You don't need to

say anything. Just listen."

Kelsey stood, and Luke's stomach curled in on itself. Was she going to agree? He wasn't sure he could let her go off with him alone.

He scooted to the end of the bench, where she'd gotten up, purse in hand. "Kelsey, don't go with him."

She spared Luke the smallest glance. "I'm going to the bathroom." She took a step toward the back.

Noah moved to block her. "Please, Kelsey. Just five minutes. I need to apologize to you. It's important for my recovery."

"She doesn't give a damn about your recovery," Luke said, fury spiraling through him. "She doesn't have to."

Kelsey turned to look at Luke, her eyes like ice. "This isn't your problem, Luke." She shot a glare toward Noah. "I don't actually care about your recovery. You need to go."

She took another step, and Noah grabbed her forearm. "*Please.*"

That was all Luke needed to see. He leapt up and planted his fist in Noah's face, hitting him in the left cheekbone and sending his head snapping back.

Noah let go of Kelsey, and she gasped, her hand flying to her mouth. Her gaze turned to Luke, but he was only seeing her from the corner of his eye. He was focused on Noah, who was massaging his cheek. Luke moved toward him. Noah took a step back.

Luke's lip curled. "Not too fun being on the receiving end, is it?"

"Luke, *stop.*" Kelsey's voice broke through his angry haze.

He didn't look at her, just kept glaring at Noah. "He deserves that and so much more."

"Luke!"

Finally, he turned his head and saw the anguish and pain in her gaze. "No one deserves that." She shook her head, her eyes wide. Sliding her purse strap over her shoulder, she cut around them and walked out.

Noah started after her, but Cam, who must've gotten up from the booth, stepped between him and the door. Cam glowered at him. "Let her go."

"I'm calling 9-1-1," Brooke said. "He's violating the restraining order. And his parole."

Panic flooded Noah's gaze. He dashed around Cam and fled the pub. Luke lurched forward, intending to follow him, but Cam put his hand on his forearm. "Don't do something you'll regret. Let's call the police, and we'll sort this out. You shouldn't have hit him."

Probably not. He shook his hand out, suddenly feeling the pain in his knuckles. He locked eyes with his older brother. "I *don't* regret that."

Cam nodded slowly. "I get it."

Luke stared at the door, aware that the entire pub had gone quiet. He reached for his phone in his back pocket but remembered he'd set it on the table when he'd sat down. He snatched it up and texted Kelsey, telling her to be careful because Noah was out there. He also said they were waiting for the police to arrive. Finally, he asked her to call or text him back. Worry and fear arced through him. He wanted to go after her, to make sure she was safe.

Fuck it. He could do that, and the police could talk to Cam and Brooke about what had happened.

Except the police walked in at that moment, and for the next half hour, the only place he went was crazy as he thought of Noah out there—maybe with Kelsey.

Chapter Seventeen
✿

KELSEY RUSHED FROM the pub without thinking where to go. She'd just wanted to get out of that situation. Seeing Noah made her feel trapped and helpless. That was why she'd gotten up to escape to the bathroom—somewhere, anywhere away from that.

Then Luke had hit him. The sight and sound of his fist hitting Noah's flesh didn't carry the sheen of vengeance she'd thought it would. No, it only reminded her of the abuse Noah had rained upon her when he'd been too angry to control himself.

The cool night breeze blew her hair back from her face and made her think for a moment. Making a decision, she strode to Luke's house and jumped in her car. She didn't know where she was going. She just knew she wanted to keep moving. She put the window down. The air kept her from losing it.

Did she think that Luke was like Noah? Rationally, she knew him hitting her ex was an emotional response and that he wouldn't ever do that to her. But did she really *know* that? Did *he* really know that? Noah had told her more than once that he didn't even recognize himself when he hit her, that it was like a demon had taken over his body.

She did know that it was a lack of control, and control was the one thing she wouldn't relinquish, not when she'd fought so hard to gain it back.

Her phone had pinged several times, but she ignored

it. After fifteen minutes or so, she pulled off the highway outside town into the parking lot of the state park near the river. She pulled her phone from her purse and read the texts from Luke.

Noah left right after you. Be careful.

We called the police.

Please call me back.

She stared at the phone, wanting to call him but also needing time to think, to process seeing Noah again. There'd been a moment when she'd wanted to go with him. She could see that he was tormented, and, as always, she wanted to ease his suffering. How many times had she comforted *him* after he'd become violent? God, it was a sick cycle.

His mother had said he was in counseling, that he was doing well. Maybe talking to Kelsey would help him.

A text appeared on the screen, but it wasn't a number in her phone, nor did she recognize it other than it had a Washington area code.

Kelsey, it's Noah. I really need to talk to you. Five minutes. I want to apologize. You deserve to hear that from me and so much more. Not the kind of apologies I gave you before. I'm an abuser. I need help and I'm getting it. None of it was your fault. Sending me to jail was the best thing you could've done for me.

She began to shake as emotion welled inside her. He was saying all the things she'd longed to hear.

Again, she considered it. Headlights flashed in the parking lot, startling her. The car drove up near hers— just two spots away in the corner.

She put her hand on the ignition, intending to leave, but a figure came toward her car and in the light from the lamp in the parking lot, she recognized that it was Noah. Apprehension raced through her as he approached her open window.

"Kelsey? Can we please talk? Did you get my text?"

She clutched the steering wheel as if it could be used as a weapon. "How did you find me?"

"I saw you driving in town, and I followed you."

She turned the key, and he held up his hands in supplication. "Kelsey, wait! Please. Just listen to me. I'm so sorry. So very sorry." Tears streaked from his eyes, and his shoulders shook.

She'd seen him do this before. His show of regret wouldn't bend her.

But then he stopped, sucking in a deep, harsh breath. "No, I won't do that to you." He wiped his hands over his eyes and straightened. "You deserve better."

"I do," she said softly, surprised that she could talk. "You shouldn't have come here. If you wanted to apologize—or whatever—you could've sent me a letter."

"I could've. My mom called you. She said you were pretty harsh."

Kelsey turned her head as anger ignited inside her. "I think I have the right to be whatever I damn well please."

He sucked his lower lip in, a familiar tic that took her back to the years they'd spent together. She'd once found it terribly sexy, alluring. It reminded her of better times.

"I'm sorry. You do. You can be harsh, cruel, whatever you want. You can even hit me if it would make you feel better."

And there it was. The retaliation she'd dreamt about in her darkest moments. But at the pub, she'd realized she didn't want revenge. She just wanted closure.

"I don't want to do that. Say what you want to say so

that I can go."

He stepped closer, and she resisted the urge to back the car up and drive away. She told herself she could at any moment. "Like I said, I'm in counseling and I'm doing better. I'm learning a lot about myself and how to function in a relationship."

"Do you think you can? Function in a relationship? How will you keep from hitting the next woman?"

He looked away briefly. "I don't know yet. It's a process. But I know it's my problem, and that's a step in the right direction, isn't it?"

She supposed so. It was certainly better than him blaming her, which he'd done. She didn't answer him. Sitting here listening was the most she would give him.

He gave her a familiar puppy dog look, one that used to make her smile. "I wondered if you could ever find a way to forgive me?"

Oh, this she wanted to answer. This was what she'd worked so hard on, but not in the way he probably imagined.

She opened the door sharply, making him step back. Adrenaline pushed her out of the car to face him. She kept one hand on the car, gripping the door. "I *have* forgiven you, Noah. But not for you. For *me*. Forgiveness is for the forgiver. I don't care if you feel better or if you're healing. I only care that *I* feel better, that *I'm* healing. And I am. Forgiving you helped me do that. Letting go of the anger and pain in my heart so that I could maybe find happiness."

He swallowed, his Adam's apple bobbing. "Have you found that?"

"I'm working on it."

He moved closer, and she smelled bourbon—his liquor of choice—on his breath. "With the guy at the pub?"

She heard something in his tone. Something that gave her pause. "It's none of your business." She climbed back into the car, thinking she never should've gotten out in the first place. But she hadn't been thinking clearly. If she were, she wouldn't even be here. "I'm going now."

"Wait, please!"

"I'm done, Noah."

He reached into the car and grabbed her wrist, his fingers closing around her flesh. She ripped her arm from his grasp and threw the car in reverse, the tires squealing as she hit the gas.

Without looking back, she pulled out of the parking lot and drove toward town. God, she was an idiot! Why had she stayed there to listen to him? She should've left the moment she'd seen him walking to the car. Was she ever going to be free of him? Could she find the happiness she wanted, that she deserved?

In that moment, she just didn't know.

&

THE COLD NIGHT air should've chilled Luke, but he was numb. In mind and body. As soon as the police had let him leave The Arch and Vine, he'd walked all over, trying to find Kelsey. She wasn't responding to his texts, and he was terrified for her. Her car was gone from his driveway, and it wasn't in her parking lot. Her apartment was dark.

He was desperate to find her, and now, back at his house, he simply stood on his porch and stared into the darkness, feeling utterly helpless.

His phone, clutched in his grasp as it had been all night, pinged. He lifted it, screen up, and saw the text was from Cam asking if he'd found Kelsey yet. Luke typed in "No" and hit Send. Cam and Brooke had walked with him at first, trying to talk him off the ledge of despair. He'd finally told them he needed to be alone, perhaps not in the kindest way. It had gone something like: "Leave me the hell alone. I'll call you if I need your 'help.'"

He winced at the memory but shoved it away, because, by far, it wasn't the worst thing that had happened tonight. He kept reliving that moment at the pub over and over. Noah touched her; Luke reacted; Kelsey looked at him in fear.

He started moving again, pacing across the porch. Why wasn't she responding to his texts? He'd sent more after finishing with the police. Even though she hadn't reported Noah's restraining order violation, which was required to press charges, they were still looking for him in town. And until Luke heard from Kelsey, his insides would continue to feel like they were drowning in acid.

If Noah had somehow found her… Luke would never forgive himself.

The sound of a car pulling onto the street made him pivot. He stepped off the porch onto the stairs. The car slowed and turned. It was Kelsey.

Relief rushed over him, and his body collapsed. He dropped down and sat on the edge of the porch.

She turned the car off and came toward him, moving faster as she got closer. She paused at the bottom of the steps. "Are you all right?"

"No." His voice creaked with emotion. "Are you? Please tell me—" He snapped his mouth shut and looked away.

"I'm fine."

He peeked at her, afraid to see...what? He didn't know.

She moved forward and stood before him. "Why are you sitting there?"

He felt defensive. Raw. "Why didn't you return my texts?"

"I had to think. I'm sorry." She shook her head and brought her hand to her chest. "I'm so stupid."

He stood, frustrated that she would demean herself. "Don't say that. I'm the stupid one. I'm so sorry about what happened. I scared you, didn't I?"

She nodded. "You...surprised me."

Cam had been right. Luke regretted what he'd done. "I wasn't thinking. I only wanted to protect you. I hope you know that. I would never—"

She rushed forward and kissed him, cutting off his words. It was fast and hard. "I know you wouldn't. I just needed to think things through, to process everything. Seeing Noah was a shock."

He curled his arm around her waist and held her close. He never wanted to let go. "I bet."

She tipped her head down, resting her forehead against his shoulder. "He followed me, and I let him talk to me." Her voice was low and dark, tainted with a horrid emotion. It was self-loathing, he realized. "He apologized and asked me to forgive him. I explained that I already had." She lifted her gaze to his. "That was part of my therapy—learning to forgive myself, which included forgiving him. I didn't want to carry that burden any longer. But I still am, just in a different form. I've been so afraid to open myself up, to let myself feel love."

His throat tightened. "I understand. I've been afraid too, just for very different reasons. I've held myself back in the fear that I might hurt you."

"I know. And I've kept you at arm's length—emotionally—in the fear that I might get hurt. But I don't want to do that anymore, Luke. I'm in love with you. I feel it, I know it, I *want* it."

Joy lifted his soul. "I love you too. I didn't recognize it at first—it sort of snuck up on me. There's just something about you, about us, that's…right."

She nodded, her mouth curving into the brightest smile. "*So* right. I feel exactly the same. It's like a song you hear for the first time. You like it, but with each listen you realize you can't stop, that you're in love with it."

"*Yes.*" He kissed her, their lips sliding over each other for a brief, wondrous moment before he continued. "You're the song in my heart, and I'll be damned if I knew there was one in there."

She laughed softly, then sobered, looking into his eyes. "I hope you don't get tired of it."

"I can't predict the future, but I don't think I will. Just the thought of that fills me with agony." He framed her face in his hands and kissed her again. "You're cold."

She pressed herself against his chest, hugging him tight. "So are you. We should go inside."

He swept her into his arms, eliciting a gasp from her followed by a giggle. Then he carried her into the house, where he set her down so he could lock the door.

She tossed her purse on the couch, and he picked her up again, this time bearing her toward the bedroom. She rolled her eyes at him. "I can walk."

"Doesn't mean you should." He kissed her as he lowered her to the floor next to the bed.

He didn't want to end this moment, but he wanted to know—had to know—where Noah was now. "I have to ask, where's Noah?"

She blinked up at him. "I don't know. I drove away and left him in the state park. That's where he followed me."

"Did you read my texts about him violating the restraining order and Brooke calling the police?"

"I did." She sank down on the bed, her shoulders drooping. "It's all so overwhelming. I just want him to go away. Back to Washington."

Luke sat beside her and took her hand. "What if he doesn't? I think you need to file a police report so they can charge him with violating the restraining order."

She was quiet for a moment and stared straight ahead. Luke knew she loved him, but her silence was freaking him out a little.

At last, she turned her head to look at him. "Okay. Can I do it in the morning? I'm exhausted, and I just want you to hold me."

That he could do. "With pleasure." He gathered her into his arms and kissed her forehead. She nuzzled into him, hugging him around the waist and laying her head against his collarbone.

After a minute, she raised her head to kiss him. Softly at first, brief touches of lips and then tongue. She curled her hand around his neck and kissed him long and deep.

She pulled back and locked her gaze with his. "Make love to me, Luke."

The long-ago echo of hearing those same words from Paige pulled at the back of his mind. With her, he'd felt a moment of panic, but now he only felt peace. And overwhelming desire for this woman who'd captured his heart.

He cupped her head and kissed her again, tugging her onto his lap. She pivoted, straddling him, and immediately began pulling at his clothing, trading garments until they were both nude. Luke began an assault on her body with his hands, lips, and tongue until she was panting and writhing beneath him. After insisting on helping him don a condom, she clasped his cock. Her fingers encircled the base before working up then down, bringing him to the edge of release.

"Kelsey, let me—"

She devoured his request with her mouth and guided him into her wet sheath. When he was buried deep, she wrapped her legs around his waist and begged him to move.

He went slowly at first, stroking her hair and face and looking into the pale blue ecstasy burning in her gaze. The deeper he stroked, the lower she moaned. Her eyelids fluttered, and she surrendered, closing her eyes as her orgasm swept through her.

He held her tight, memorizing the curve of her cheek and the exact pink of her lips. So this was what love felt like. True, searing love that scored into your soul.

Like her, he yielded—not just to his body but to the incandescent emotion flowing through him. He gave her everything he had, and when they were finished, he held her close to his heart.

"Thank you," she murmured. "I have never felt so safe. So protected."

As she fell asleep in his arms, he vowed to make sure she felt that way forever.

Chapter Eighteen
ও ঌ

THE SMELL OF bacon filled the house as Luke plated breakfast. Kelsey would have just enough time to eat before dashing off to the library. They'd slept a bit late and then showered together, which perhaps hadn't been the most time-saving enterprise.

He smiled to himself, setting breakfast on the table and pouring Kelsey's coffee into a travel mug. She breezed into the kitchen, looking fresh and beautiful. She'd pulled her hair into a long ponytail and was dressed in a knee-length denim skirt, cute striped sweater, and sexy boots that made him want to steer her right back into the bedroom.

"You look too good to go to work," Luke said, devouring her with his eyes.

She laughed. "You are a naughty boy, Luke Westcott."

He was so glad to see her happy this morning. Last night had been tough. And it wasn't really over. Noah was still out there, maybe even in Ribbon Ridge. What if he showed up at the library this morning?

He hated to pop the joyous bubble that seemed to be surrounding them, but he had to broach the subject. "Are you going to call the police about Noah?"

She sat down and dug into her breakfast of scrambled eggs and bacon. "I will after I get to work."

Luke swallowed his frustration along with a piece of bacon. He wanted to say more but also didn't want to get into an argument. He reached over and touched her arm. "I don't want to see you get hurt. You get that, right?"

"Of course I do." She blinked at him before dropping her gaze to her plate.

Luke was getting a weird vibe from her. He tried to focus on eating his breakfast. After a minute, he glanced over at her and noticed that she wasn't wearing her bracelet. "Hey, where's your bracelet?"

She turned her left wrist over. "Oh yeah." She blanched. "I can't find it. I was hoping you wouldn't notice. I'm sure it'll turn up."

She kept her focus on her plate, which he also found odd. What was going on with her?

She looked up at the clock on the microwave. "Yikes, I need to go." She pushed her half-eaten breakfast away and stood.

He got up with her. "Hey, what's wrong?"

She looked away, for some reason unable—or unwilling—to meet his gaze. "Something happened when I saw Noah last night." She focused on him then, her eyes tormented. "I don't want you to be upset. It was nothing. He tried to grab my wrist. I drove away. End of story."

She hadn't told him the truth last night. She hadn't wanted him to know that Noah had gotten physical. "Were you afraid I'd go after him if you told me what happened?"

She took a moment to answer. "I don't know. Maybe?" She laid her palm against his collarbone. "I'm sorry I didn't tell you. I need to go. Can we continue this later?"

He nodded, feeling as though he were in a fog. She kissed him before grabbing her coffee from the table.

She plucked her purse from the couch and waved at him before she left.

Luke tried to finish his breakfast but couldn't shake the feeling of anxiety rattling his frame. If Noah had clasped her wrist and she was now missing her bracelet, maybe she'd lost it at the park. It was a long shot, but he needed some fresh air to clear his head anyway. He put his boots on and threw on a sweatshirt before snagging his keys from the hook and heading out.

Driving to the state park, he wondered if there was more to Kelsey's behavior than simply not telling him about Noah grabbing her. Luke hated thinking that she was afraid of his reaction.

He parked in the lot and stepped out of his Jeep. He stood there a moment and contemplated where to start looking. He should've asked for more information about where Kelsey had met Noah. He pulled his phone from his pocket and texted her. She didn't immediately respond.

While he waited, he walked to the edge of the parking lot and looked down toward the river. There was quite a slope unless you went to the left and took the path. Something near the water's edge drew his attention. A shoe. He tipped his head to the side and squinted, but couldn't see beyond the black boot.

He turned and strode to the path, walking quickly to the bottom. The path continued to the left, but he veered right through the low shrubbery to get to the shoreline. The terrain was uneven but walkable. As he neared the boot, the appendage it was attached to came into view. The body—a large man—lay on its stomach.

Luke crept up to the man's side and knelt down.

Holy fuck.

It was Noah.

Luke pushed at Noah's shoulder. "Noah, wake up." When he didn't respond, Luke touched his neck. The flesh was like ice, and Luke's search for a pulse came up empty.

Shit, shit, shit. Luke's blood ran cold. He looked at Noah's face, gray and hard in death, absurdly wishing the man could tell him what had happened. Then he saw the dark red stain on Noah's head.

Luke glanced around looking for what might've caused the wound and instantly saw the jagged rock nearby. Without thinking, he picked it up. When he saw blood, he dropped it as panic surged in his chest.

What the hell had happened? Was this why Kelsey had seemed agitated? Why she'd ignored him last night? He needed to talk to her. Pulling out his phone again, he saw that she still hadn't responded. *Dammit.*

He stood up and looked toward the path, where a jogger was running along the water, about to turn uphill toward the parking lot. He nodded in greeting at Luke.

Well, now he had to call the police.

Not that he wouldn't have, but he'd really hoped to talk to Kelsey first.

Luke dialed 911 and reported what he'd found. What had happened here last night? Suddenly, Kelsey's odd behavior that morning took on a sinister tone. He didn't for a moment think she'd killed Noah on purpose. She wasn't a murderer. If she *was* involved, Luke knew it had to have been self-defense.

The sound of sirens filled the air as Ribbon Ridge's police showed up, followed by a county deputy. Luke waved at them from the riverbank, and three officers came down to survey the scene.

Things happened very quickly then as the cops talked on their radios. An officer from Ribbon Ridge spoke to

Luke and took notes. "So you knew this guy?" he asked Luke.

Luke nodded. "Yes. I mean, not really. He's my girlfriend's ex. He came into The Arch and Vine last night. She has a restraining order against him, and I'm pretty sure his being here violates his parole. He just got out of prison a few weeks ago."

"I see. This sounds familiar. You called the police last night?"

"Not me. My brother's fiancé."

"What happened at the pub last night?"

Shit. They already knew Luke had decked Noah. That wasn't going to look good. "He got too close to Kelsey—he touched her, actually. I, uh, I hit him." His knuckles twitched. "He left shortly after."

"Right. Okay, well, I think we're good for now. Don't go too far. I'm sure we'll have more questions."

Luke shook his hand. "Sure. I'm just going to head back into town."

The officer nodded, and Luke walked up to his car. His hands shook as he dug his keys from his pocket. He quickly climbed into his Jeep and drove toward the library, hoping Kelsey's world wasn't about to explode.

❧

STELLA, THE FIFTY-SOMETHING owner of one of Ribbon Ridge's coffee shops, took the book from Kelsey after she'd checked it out. "Thanks for the recommendation."

Kelsey smiled. "I hope you like it."

"I'll let you know if I don't next time you stop in for a latte." She winked at Kelsey before turning and leaving.

Kelsey exhaled and glanced around. There were still a few people in the library, but it had been a busy day so far, and Kelsey would gratefully take a lull, even if it was just for a few minutes. After the long day at the vineyard yesterday, Kelsey had given Marci the day off. However, it was becoming clearer that the library needed two people on the weekends. Time to revisit the budget and maybe write a grant proposal.

The sound of the door opening drew Kelsey's attention. She turned her head and saw Luke coming in. The smile that rose to her lips died almost immediately. His eyes were dark, and his face was creased with worry.

He came right toward her. "We need to talk. Please tell me Marci's here so we can go upstairs."

Alarm seared through Kelsey's chest. "She isn't. What's the matter? You're freaking me out."

He glanced around, noting the patrons browsing the shelves and the two children sitting in the reading nook. He touched Kelsey's arm and led her back behind the counter. When he looked into her eyes, she could see the concern running rampant through him, along with something else. Something that made her spine tingle with apprehension.

"I went to the park to look for your bracelet." His frigid tone stoked her fear.

"Did you find it?"

He shook his head. "No. But I found Noah." He paused, scaring her even more with the grim set of his mouth. "Kelsey, he's dead."

Her knees buckled, and she sank to the floor. Luke helped her up, practically lifting her, and set her in the chair behind her desk. "You didn't know."

Noah was dead? She looked at Luke, processing what he'd said. "You thought I did?"

"I wasn't sure." The furrows in his brow carved deeper. "You were acting strange this morning. You said he tried to grab you... I wouldn't blame you."

Oh God. He thought she'd killed him. "He was fine when I left the park. I swear." Panic started to rise in her throat. If her own boyfriend thought she could do that, what would the police say? "Did you call the police?"

"I had to." He gave his head a shake. "I would have anyway, but a jogger saw me with the body. Kelsey, they're going to come here and question you. You need to be ready."

It was as if she was standing outside in subzero temperatures, an icy wind blowing over her suddenly hard and brittle body. She was afraid the slightest movement would make her shatter.

She tried to parse through the emotions and thoughts battering through her. Noah was dead. Luke thought she might've done it. The police would be coming to talk to her.

"Excuse me," a small voice said from beyond her desk. "Can you help me find more Bad Kitty books?"

Right. She was also at work.

Summoning a calm she didn't remotely feel, she stood and gave the boy—he was maybe eight years old—a weak smile. "Sure. Come on."

As she walked to the children's area with the little boy, she felt Luke's stare boring through her back. Did he believe her when she'd said that Noah had been fine? She began to shake.

With great effort, she focused on locating the books the boy was looking for. He beamed and immediately plucked one from the shelf before plopping down on the floor and reading. Kelsey stood there and let the joy of this boy's discovery take away the despair curdling inside her, if only for a moment.

She heard the door again and was afraid to turn in case it was the police. She'd wanted more information from Luke. Reluctantly, she pivoted and her heart sank as she watched the two officers move inside. They made eye contact with Luke, whose jaw was stiff, his muscles clearly tense. At least to her.

Kelsey walked toward them, her legs like jelly.

"Good afternoon," one of the officers said. "I'm Officer Hendricks and this is Officer Talbot." He gestured to the other cop. "We're here to talk with you about Noah Putnam." Hendricks glanced toward Luke before returning his focus to Kelsey. "I take it you know he's dead?"

Kelsey nodded. "Let's go back here." She led the officers behind her desk to get as far away from any of the patrons as possible. One of them had noticed the police coming in and was now watching the situation. Kelsey tried to ignore that.

"Yes, Luke told me about Noah." It suddenly hit her—this man she'd known for almost eight years, a man she'd loved and at one time expected to spend her life with, this man who'd broken her heart and her trust in every way possible, was dead. Emotion overwhelmed her, and she began to cry, great heaving sobs. She turned away from the library and faced the back wall.

Someone—Luke, she realized—handed her a tissue. It took her a moment to pull herself together. She saw that the officers were watching her with sympathy. That was nice.

She blew her nose and reached for another tissue.

"I'm sorry. I'm just so shocked."

"Noah was your ex-boyfriend?" Hendricks asked.

Kelsey nodded. "Yes. You must also know that he abused me, that he recently got out of jail after serving a sentence for that abuse."

"Yes, we're aware of his criminal history," Talbot said. "We're also aware that he came to town looking for you last night and found you at The Arch and Vine."

"Yes." She glanced toward Luke, thinking of how he'd hit Noah. Luke had told her last night that they'd called the police to report Noah's violation of his parole and the restraining order. They had to know he'd hit Noah, and that couldn't look good. Wait, did she think Luke could've done more?

No, that wasn't possible. Noah had been perfectly fine—although drunk—when she'd left him last night, and she'd gone directly to Luke's house where they'd been together all night. Except she'd fallen into a hard, dreamless sleep. Could Luke have left?

She shook her head. This wasn't helping matters.

Officer Talbot pulled out a small tablet and a stylus. "Can you tell us what happened after you left The Arch and Vine?"

She glanced toward Luke, but his gaze was inscrutable. What was he thinking? Why was she so nervous? She hadn't done anything. "I drove around. I was upset about seeing Noah again."

"What happened when you drove around?" Talbot asked.

The question seemed pointed. Like they already knew… And if they looked at Noah's phone, they'd see his texts asking to meet her. "He followed me to the state park. We talked for a few minutes."

Officer Hendricks tipped his head to the side. "I don't suppose you own a silver bracelet with a book charm?"

She heard her intake of breath as if someone else had done it and instantly wished she could take it back. But what would be the point in lying? They'd figure out it was hers. "Yes."

Her voice sounded so small, so frightened.

"Where did you find it?" Luke's question was gruff. Kelsey still couldn't read his eyes, but the pitch of his brows and the tight set of his features told her enough.

"With the body," Hendricks answered.

Kelsey felt as if the floor beneath her was disintegrating and she was about to tumble into an abyss.

"Miss McDade, we still have some investigation to do, but it looks like Mr. Putnam was perhaps hit with a rock," Talbot said.

She started to shake her head. Everything went fuzzy, like she was submerged in water. Even the sounds around her were muffled.

Until Luke spoke.

"I hit him at the pub because he'd grabbed Kelsey. He must've gotten her bracelet then," Luke said, his voice deep and clear. "After Kelsey got back to my house, I went to the park to confront him. We argued and things got physical. I hit him with the rock in self-defense. You'll find my fingerprints on it."

Kelsey turned her head in shock. He *had* left last night? What had he hoped to accomplish?

Talbot frowned as he exchanged looks with Hendricks. "You're saying you killed him?"

"I'm saying I hit him with the rock. And I left. Not my finest moment." He didn't look at Kelsey despite her silently begging him to do so. What was happening?

"Excuse me," a feminine voice said from the counter. "I'm sorry to interrupt, but we need to go, and we wanted to check out these Bad Kitty books."

Kelsey stared at her for a moment before pulling herself from the nightmare unfolding before her. She looked at the officers. "Give me a minute."

"Why don't we go to the station," Luke said, his voice flat. "I'll answer your questions there."

"Okay," Hendricks said. He turned to Kelsey. "Can you join us there as soon as possible?"

She nodded. "I'll close up as soon as I can." Luke started for the door with the officers following behind him. "Wait," Kelsey said. "Is he under arrest?"

Officer Talbot sent her a grim look. "Not yet."

Yet. Which meant it was possible.

"Luke, I'll bring Aubrey Archer," she called after him, but Luke didn't turn.

As she watched them leave, she felt the distinct fracture of her already battered heart.

Chapter Nineteen
♥♥

AT THE POLICE station, Luke sat in a small conference room that didn't look anything like the interrogation rooms he saw on television. But then he hadn't been arrested yet.

Yet.

Shit. What was he doing?

Protecting Kelsey. He didn't think she'd done anything—he believed her when she said Noah had been fine when she'd left him at the park. But it didn't look good with the texts and the bracelet. God, the bracelet. That was a damning piece of evidence. Circumstantial, yes, but they'd be able to put Kelsey at the scene—not just from the bracelet—and she certainly had motive.

What else could Luke do but protect her?

Officer Talbot, a balding guy in his late thirties, came into the room. "You may not know this, but there's a weather camera at the park. Don't know if it'll show us anything from last night, but it might. With that in mind, can you walk us through what happened?" He sat down at the conference table.

Dread curled through Luke. He shifted in his chair. He needed to buy some time. He was sure Kelsey hadn't done this, but he didn't want her to be scrutinized by the police. Dammit, hadn't Noah put her through enough? Still, Luke wondered what had happened. Who had killed him if it wasn't Kelsey? And it sure as hell hadn't been Luke, regardless of what he was trying to pull right now.

"I need to speak with my lawyer." He cringed inwardly, certain this made the situation even worse, but not knowing what else to do.

Talbot exhaled. "Okay. You do realize you're not under arrest at this point?"

"Yes." Just as he knew his rights. "I still want to talk to my lawyer."

Talbot stood. "You can make a call."

Luke pulled his phone from his pocket. They hadn't taken anything from him. *Yet.*

He was beginning to hate that word.

Talbot left, and Luke saw that he had several texts from Kelsey. His phone had been on vibrate, and he hadn't felt it in the pocket of his sweatshirt. She was on her way to the station with Aubrey Archer.

No need to call an attorney, then.

He didn't respond to Kelsey. What could he say? Anything he typed and sent would be used against them.

Against them? Did he really think it would come to that? He set the phone on the table and dropped his head into his hands. He didn't know anything. And he didn't know when he would.

After what felt like an eternity but was maybe a quarter hour, the door opened and Aubrey came into the room. She sat down next to Luke and gave him an encouraging smile. "Hey, Luke. Nice day to be at the police station."

He narrowed his eyes at her, and she raised her hand, palm up. "Sorry," she said. "Bad attempt at levity. Listen, I'm not a criminal defense attorney, but let's see if you really need one. Can you tell me what happened?"

Luke had tried to come up with what he would say. If he told the truth, she'd know that he was innocent of anything—including using the rock in self-defense— and she'd simply relay that to the police. Wouldn't she?

He tried to calm the storm raging through him. "Where's Kelsey?"

"She's out in the waiting room. We thought it best if I came in and talked to you first."

Or did Kelsey just prefer not to see him because she thought he'd killed her ex? He supposed that was proof that *she* hadn't done it. Wait, did he really think she had? He realized he kept going back and forth. Logically, rationally, he knew she hadn't. But emotionally, he didn't know. He could see how she would do whatever necessary to protect herself against Noah. Assuming it was self-defense.

Fuck, his head was doing a number on him. He needed to talk to her. Now.

"I need to talk to *her* first."

Aubrey frowned. "I'm not sure that's a good idea. This is serious, Luke. You admitted to killing a man."

"No, I admitted to hitting him in self-defense." Which he hadn't done either. "Please get Kelsey." He stood abruptly. "Never mind. I'm not under arrest. I can do what I want."

Aubrey rose. "No. I'll get her." She gave him a wary look before leaving the room.

Luke paced as he waited for Kelsey to arrive. She walked in and slowly closed the door behind her. They stared at each other across the length of the table with maybe six feet between them.

"Should we sit?" she asked. Her voice sounded distant, unfamiliar.

"Sure." Luke sat down in the chair at the end of the table. She did the same. It was as if all the intimacy of last night had never happened.

"Luke…" She looked down briefly. When her gaze shot back up, he thought he saw moisture, and her cheeks started to flush. "Why would you go after Noah?"

"I didn't." He sounded harsh and didn't mean to. Forcing himself to take a deep breath and push some of the anxiety away, he tried again. "I didn't go after him. I just said that."

"To protect me?"

He nodded.

"Do you think—do you think I killed him?"

"No." But it was clear she'd believed that he had. And why wouldn't she when he said he was trying to protect her? "At least not on purpose."

"I told you he was fine when I left him."

"You've told me all sorts of bits and pieces and not very willingly, I might add." He ran his hand through his hair, feeling as though his control was completely slipping away. He grasped it tightly, as if his life depended on it. "I just want you to be honest with me. Please be honest with me."

She said nothing for a moment. He watched her swallow, then rise slowly to her feet. She walked the length of the table and pulled out the chair next to his. He pivoted, resting his arm on the table, using that connection as some sort of lame way to ground himself despite feeling as though the wind of anguish might sweep him away.

Without words, she took his hands in hers. Her touch was cold, but her gaze was warm. "I'm so sorry. Noah has always done a number on me. Seeing him last night made me feel like I did when I was with him. Alone. Powerless. Scared."

For a brief moment, Luke wished he *had* killed the bastard.

"After I left the pub, I couldn't think. When you hit him, all I could see, all I could *feel*, was Noah hitting me."

Luke's heart cracked. "Oh my God, Kelsey."

She squeezed his hands. "It's okay. I mean, it's not okay, but it's not you. I don't blame you. It just is what it is, and, like everything else to do with that asshole, I have to work through it and figure it out. I understand why you hit him, and I'm not mad at you for that. Just like I wouldn't be mad if you felt like you had to hit him with a rock in self-defense."

Relief stole through him, but it was short-lived. "I didn't. But *someone* did."

"So it seems. But it wasn't me. He followed me to the park and got out of his car to talk to me. I was sitting there with my window open just trying to deal with all the crap in my head. I listened to him for a minute or two, and I said I was leaving. That's when he grabbed me." She let go of Luke's hands and encircled her left wrist with her right hand. "He must've got my bracelet. I didn't even realize. Anyway, I left and I didn't look back. I drove straight to your house, and I was there all night." She took his hands again. "Just as I know you were there too. Which I will tell the police. There's no way I'm letting you confess to something you didn't do."

He scooted to the edge of his chair and lifted her hand so he could press a kiss to the back. "I don't want you to have to go through an investigation. What if they think they have enough evidence to arrest you?"

She shrugged. "I don't know. But the truth will come out. They'll find out that neither one of our fingerprints are on that rock."

Luke let out a humorless laugh. "Except mine are. I stupidly picked it up when I found Noah."

She winced, and her eyes grew wide. "Oh no."

"It's still circumstantial. And there's a video—Talbot told me—from a weather camera. Hopefully it will show that neither one of us did anything."

She slumped, and he saw the relief flooding her gaze. "Then what happened to him?"

"I have no idea, and I honestly don't care, so long as it doesn't affect us." He recalled her reaction at the library, her tears. "But I suppose it does," he said softly. "You seemed pretty upset."

Her lips curved up, not quite forming a smile. She let go of his hand and leaned forward as she touched his cheek. "I was. Noah was a big part of my life for a long time. I had to learn to grieve the loss of my hopes and dreams with him. And now that he's truly out of my life forever, I can do that in a way that I couldn't before. I think." She shook her head. "I don't know. I need to call my therapist."

"So you don't miss him?"

She looked horrified. "God, no. I mourn the loss of the man I thought he was, the man I wanted him to be, the man I suppose I was hoping he could rehabilitate himself into. I do feel bad for his family. This whole ordeal has been awful, and for it to end this way is very sad."

Luke could agree with that. "You have the kindest, most generous heart of anyone I know."

She laughed again, but it was dark and hollow. "You might not think that when I tell you a part of me is glad he's gone."

He cupped the back of her head and kissed her. "Not at all. I think you're human and amazing."

She tipped her forehead against his. "I love you."

He massaged her nape. "I love you too."

The door opened, breaking them apart. Officers Talbot and Hendricks came inside and stood at the other end of the table.

"So what the heck are you both doing here?" Hendricks asked, looking bemused. "We looked at the video and saw quite a show."

Luke let go of Kelsey's neck and held her hand tight.

Talbot set his hands on his hips. "Miss McDade, the video shows Putnam talking to you at your car. We could see that he reached in through the car window. Then you backed up and left. He spent the next several minutes pacing around the parking lot and waving his hands. He looked quite agitated."

"I'm fairly certain he was drunk," Kelsey said.

"Good to know, though the toxicology report will tell us for sure," Hendricks said. "He started walking along the edge of the parking lot, at the top of that steep slope down to the river. Then he fell over the edge."

Relief exploded inside Luke. "He fell on the rock?"

"That, or he fell and then you went and hit him with a rock. Are we really going to find your fingerprints on it?"

Some of Luke's apprehension returned. "I'm afraid so. But only because I picked it up when I found him. I saw the blood and just touched it without thinking. Sorry for messing with your crime scene."

The officers exchanged looks. "Well, we can't see what happened after he fell, but once we process everything, we should be able to confirm what happened. In the meantime, we'd like it very much if neither one of you left town."

"No problem, Officers," Kelsey said. "Ribbon Ridge is my home. There's nowhere I'd rather be."

Luke sent her a sidelong glance, and she'd turned to smile at him. They looked at each other with love. "Same here," he said.

Talbot inhaled sharply. "All right, then. You can both go whenever you'd like. But Westcott?"

"Yeah?"

"Don't pick up bloody rocks or go off hitting guys in bars, okay? It doesn't look too good. Even when the guy's a felon."

Luke saluted. "Yes, sirs."

The cops shook their heads at him, Hendricks with a faint smile, before they turned and left.

Luke stood, pulling Kelsey up with him. "Shall we go?"

"Yes, please."

"Where? Do you want to go to your apartment?"

She looked at him as if he'd lost his mind. "To your house. *Home.*"

Emotions roiled through him, but he clung to the one he wanted to feel most—love. He kissed her again before escorting her out.

ৎৡ

WHEN THEY GOT home, Kelsey was beyond exhausted, but she asked Luke if they could invite her grandmother over. Kelsey had weathered so much on her own, and now that she had family close, she wanted to embrace it.

Luke hadn't minded at all. They'd also decided to include Cam since Brooke had texted to check on Kelsey multiple times since the incident at the pub the night before.

After running to the market to fetch supplies, Kelsey threw together a salad and some scalloped potatoes while Luke roasted a pork loin. As she set the table, she realized it was the first time they were entertaining as a couple. She smiled at the thought.

Brooke and Cam arrived first, with an excellent bottle of wine, naturally. Brooke hugged Kelsey tight. "I'm so sorry to hear about everything that happened." Her brow creased as she rubbed Kelsey's shoulder.

Kelsey knew that Luke had talked to his brother after they'd gotten home and given him the scoop. "It's been an exhausting day."

Luke answered the knock on the door and welcomed Gram and George inside. Gram went straight for Kelsey and wrapped her arms around her. "Are you all right, dear?"

Kelsey had spoken to her briefly, just saying that Noah had come to town and died in a freak accident. Kelsey and Luke both hoped that all the testing the police were doing would confirm that he'd simply died in the fall. Neither could imagine anything nefarious happening in—or that close to—Ribbon Ridge.

"I'm doing fine, Gram." Surprisingly so. Luke's strength and support were like a balm to her soul.

"It helps to have Luke, doesn't it?" Gram glanced over to where he stood with George, taking his jacket.

Kelsey was unable to stifle a smile. "Did you read my mind?"

Gram chuckled. "When one is newly in love, it's

particularly easy to spot others in the same situation." She kissed Kelsey's cheek.

"Wine?" Cam called from the kitchen where he was pouring out the pinot noir he'd brought.

"Absolutely!" George went to the island, where Cam had set out the glasses. George waited until everyone had grabbed a glass before raising his and toasting, "To family."

They all chimed in and clinked their glasses together, then Kelsey began the nerve-racking task of recounting the sequence of events from when Noah had shown up at the pub.

When she'd finished, Gram shook her head. "Such a shame. I can't imagine why he thought it was a good idea to come down here."

"I think he was hoping there was still a chance for us," Kelsey said, feeling sad. "It *is* a shame because he was getting help. I really hoped he'd pull himself together."

Luke put his arm around her waist. "You are a saint."

Everyone agreed, and then they sat down to dinner. Luke opened two more bottles of wine, and by the time they were finished eating, the mood had lightened. Brooke helped Kelsey tidy up the kitchen while everyone else adjourned to the living room.

"So where do you go from here?" Brooke asked as Kelsey closed the dishwasher and set it to run later.

"First, I call my therapist tomorrow morning."

Brooke smiled encouragingly. "Good start. What about you and Luke?"

"Nothing's changed." Actually, that wasn't necessarily true. The love she felt for him had only intensified. There was still a bit of fear in the back of her mind, but she accepted that there was risk in anything worth having. "I'm in love with him, and I hope we're together for a long time."

Brooke grinned. "I hope you're together forever! If you get married, we'll be sisters-in-law!"

Kelsey laughed. "I suppose so. But let's not get ahead of ourselves." She was quite content to stay the current course and see where it took them.

Later, after everyone had gone home, Kelsey snuggled back up against Luke in bed. The exhaustion she'd managed to keep at bay swept over her, and she couldn't keep her eyelids open.

He wrapped his arms around her and held her close to his warm chest. "Kels?"

She didn't open her eyes. "Mmm?"

"Maybe now isn't the best time to ask, but I'd like you to stay here permanently. If you're ready."

She was suddenly quite awake. Rolling in his embrace, she opened her eyes and looked up at him. Though it was dark, she could just make out his features. "I think I am." Her answer surprised her as much as him—if the subtle rounding of his eyes meant that he was surprised. And she thought it did. She curled her arm around his neck. "Did you think I'd say no?"

"I thought you'd at least say you needed to think about it."

"I don't. I'll give notice on my crappy apartment tomorrow." Happiness unfurled inside her, and she had to giggle to let it out before she exploded.

"Is that joy because you're giving notice or because you're coming to live here?"

She tugged at the hair at his nape. "It's joy because of you. Because of what we've found together. Because of what the future has in store." She pulled his head down

So Right

and kissed him. "I love you so much."

"And I love you." He kissed her again, and she knew that nothing in her life had ever felt so right.

Epilogue
❧

Thanksgiving, Ribbon Ridge

THERE WERE SO many people at the Archers' Thanksgiving dinner that they were spread out over three rooms and just as many tables. There were Archers and Westcotts, and children and George and Ruby, and a few friends, such as Crystal. It was a massive undertaking, but Luke knew that Rob and Emily Archer were delighted to do it. And between seven children and their spouses, plus the added guests, they had plenty of hands on deck. Luke and Kelsey had brought yams and an apple pie. It turned out Kelsey was an excellent baker. If he wasn't careful, he'd be twice his size come next year.

Seated at the large table in the kitchen, he stretched his legs out after dinner, satisfied in every way possible. He draped his arm across the back of Kelsey's chair beside him and let his fingers graze her shoulder. The diamond ring in his pocket felt heavy, which was silly. It wasn't really—he was just exceedingly aware of its presence.

And unbearably excited about it.

He looked over at Kelsey and grinned like an idiot. As if she could feel his stare, she turned her head. A bemused expression stole over her features. "What?"

He shook his head. "Later." He planned to pop the question before dessert so that they could announce their happy news over pie.

Assuming she said yes. He realized it was fast, but he wanted to spend his life with her. And he wanted everyone to know it.

Last week, they'd closed the case on Noah's death, ruling it an accident. The evidence had revealed that he'd fallen down the hill and struck his head on the rock. The result had been a massive brain hemorrhage, and he'd died almost immediately. He'd also been—literally—fall-down drunk. With that behind them, it seemed they had a fresh beginning, and he was eager to move forward.

Rob Archer came into the kitchen from the dining room. "Can everybody come into the living room? We want to say a few things." He smiled as he gestured through another doorway to the great room.

Luke stood and held Kelsey's chair. They moved as a group into the living room, passing Rob on their way. Taking stock of everyone in the room, there had to be about thirty people, including the toddlers and babies.

Rob came in then and stood near the massive stone fireplace. "Thanks for coming today. It's our pleasure to share Thanksgiving with all of you. We're truly honored by your presence. And none more than my good friend George, who has something he'd like to say."

George had been standing off to the side with Ruby. He took her hand, and they walked together to the fireplace. Luke had a pretty good idea what was going to come next, and he couldn't have been more thrilled.

Putting his arm around Ruby, George looked around the room. "I've known most of you a long time. Which means you know me too. Or at least you think you do." He chuckled as he glanced down at Ruby and gave her a squeeze. "This might surprise you—it sure surprised me, and in the best way possible." He grinned much the way Luke had a few moments ago in the kitchen. "This lovely young thing standing beside me has agreed to be my wife."

No one would ever know if he meant to say more, because the room simply erupted in cheers and excitement. One of the babies started to cry.

When Kelsey didn't rush forward to hug her grandma, Luke turned to her and asked, "Did you know about this?"

She nodded, and he saw tears in her eyes. "She called me this morning right after he proposed. I think she wanted my permission." She laughed as she swiped her fingers beneath her eyes.

Luke hugged her and kissed her forehead. His proposal could wait. He didn't want to take a moment of the spotlight away from George and Ruby.

After everyone had finished mobbing the newly engaged couple, Luke and Kelsey took their turn. Luke shook George's hand, but George pulled him into a fierce bear hug instead.

"I figure we're family now, right?" He thumped Luke's back before pulling away.

Luke coughed. "Good Lord, George. How much are you bench-pressing these days?" He grinned at the older man, who laughed in return.

Luke waited until Kelsey and her grandmother finished embracing before giving Ruby a hug too. "I'm so happy for you both."

"Thank you. It's quite a thing, isn't it?" She put her arm around Kelsey and pulled her close. "And won't Kelsey look lovely as my maid of honor?" She kissed Kelsey's cheek.

Luke couldn't dispute that. Kelsey looked lovely every single minute of every single day. "She certainly will."

"I've decided to take a page from Kelsey's book and cut back my hours at The Arch and Vine," George called out, effectively silencing the group. "Sorry, but it's time to embrace at least semiretirement so I can enjoy my bride."

"I think that's great," Luke said to Kelsey. She'd gone down to working just two days a week at the pub, plus she'd help out as necessary, though that hadn't come up yet. They'd both been surprised to realize they didn't like working as much now that they'd found each other.

Kelsey smiled up at him. "Right? I knew you'd get it."

After gorging themselves on five kinds of pie, Luke and Kelsey finally went home, where Luke immediately stripped and put on athletic shorts and a roomy T-shirt. "I need fat clothes," he said.

Kelsey laughed. "Hey, I did the same thing. I just went straight for pajamas, though."

He arched a brow at her. "You think you're going to wear those for long?"

"At least until you digest a little!"

"Good point. Let's see what we can hunt up on Netflix." He turned and went into the living room.

A few minutes later, Kelsey joined him, but she didn't sit. He turned to look at her standing at the end of the couch, staring at him, the chinos he'd been wearing in her hand.

She looked... He wasn't sure what she looked, but it wasn't necessarily good.

He muted the TV and turned to face her. "What's

wrong?"

She hesitated before saying, "I, uh, you left your pants on the bed. I was going to hang them up for you." With her free hand, she held up her thumb and forefinger. Which held the diamond ring he'd planned to give her.

"Shit." Really? That's what he said? He jumped up. "I mean… Oops. I forgot that was in there."

"I see."

He laughed then, amused by the absurdity of the situation and his idiocy. "I'm not sure *how* I forgot, since I'd been planning to give it to you." He added, "Obviously," in case that needed to be said.

"When?"

"After dinner. Before dessert. Pretty much when George announced his engagement to your grandma." He scrubbed his hand over his jaw. "I didn't want to steal their thunder, so I decided to wait."

Her mouth formed an O, but no sound came out. She held it out. "Here. You're amazing. I love you."

He realized there would be no better time than the present. He took the ring from her and stepped toward her, dropping to one knee. "Kelsey McDade, you've made me happier than I ever imagined. I never thought I'd find someone I'd want to share my life with. You're my lover, my best friend, my soul mate. Will you marry me?"

She stared at him, her mouth open. At last, she nodded, slowly at first and then increasingly faster. He actually feared she might give herself whiplash.

"So that's a yes, then?"

She stuck her left hand out, and he slipped the ring on her finger. It was a little too big, unfortunately. "We'll get it sized," he said.

She stared at it, holding her hand flat and then bringing it closer to her face. "Is this real?"

"Um, yes?" Of all the reactions he'd been expecting, *that* wasn't it.

She laughed, then clapped her hand over her mouth. The diamond sparkled on her finger. She pulled her hand away and looked at the ring again. "That's not what I meant. What I *meant* is this"—she looked down at him, her eyes pale and glistening, and gestured to him and back to her—"is *this* real?"

He stood and clasped her waist. "Absolutely," he said softly.

She wrapped her arms around his neck and kissed him. "Can we keep this to ourselves? Just for a bit. The weekend. I loved that you wanted my grandma and George to enjoy the spotlight. You are the best of men."

He smiled down at her and smoothed her hair back from her face. "Whatever makes you happy."

She tipped her head to the side, her mouth curving into a gorgeous grin. "That's easy. You."

The end

Thank You!
❦

Thank you so much for reading *So Right*, book two in the So Hot series! I hope you enjoyed your stay in Ribbon Ridge and that you'll come back for the third and final book, *So Wrong*, featuring Jamie Westcott and Crystal Donovan. In the meantime, you can catch up with the Archer family in the seven book Ribbon Ridge series.

Ribbon Ridge is a fictional town based on several cities and towns dotting the Willamette Valley between Portland and the Oregon Coast. It's pinot noir wine country, very beautiful and picturesque, and a short drive from where I live. My brother actually dwells right in the heart of it in a tiny town with no stoplights. There is, however, an amazing antique mall in an historic schoolhouse (and apparently seven Pokestops).

Be sure to visit my Facebook (darcyburkefans) for the latest information, follow me on Twitter (@darcyburke), check out images of the northern Willamette Valley and other things that inspired this series on Pinterest (darcyburkewrite), and sign up for my newsletter at darcyburke.com so you'll know exactly when my next book is available.

Thank you again for reading and for your support! xo

Books by Darcy Burke

Contemporary Romance

Ribbon Ridge

Where the Heart Is (a prequel novella)
Only in My Dreams
Yours to Hold
When Love Happens
The Idea of You
When We Kiss
You're Still the One

Ribbon Ridge: So Hot

So Good
So Right
So Wrong

Historical Romance

The Untouchables

The Forbidden Duke
The Duke of Daring
The Duke of Deception
The Duke of Desire
The Duke of Defiance
The Duke of Danger
The Duke of Ice
The Duke of Ruin
The Duke of Lies
The Duke of Seduction
The Duke of Kisses

Secrets and Scandals

Her Wicked Ways
His Wicked Heart
To Seduce a Scoundrel
To Love a Thief (a novella)
Never Love a Scoundrel
Scoundrel Ever After

Legendary Rogues

Lady of Desire
Romancing the Earl
Lord of Fortune
Captivating the Scoundrel

Acknowledgments

Several professionals helped with this book, and I am deeply grateful for their expertise. Any errors are mine. Thank you Heather Durham for your assistance with the crime scene specifics and also, for being a wonderful friend. Thanks to my husband Steve for all the legal stuff. And thank you to Rachel Grant for her archaeological knowledge and help with the map situation. If you haven't read her books, you totally should. I LOVE them.

Thank you to Elisabeth Naughton and Rachel (again) for their help with this book. I absolutely cherish our time together and appreciate you both from the bottom of my heart.

As always, endless love and thanks to my beautiful family. You make every day the best day ever.

SO GOOD
So Hot, Book One

"...worth the read with its well-written words, beautiful descriptions, and likeable characters. Brooke is smart, attractive, and knows her wine. Cam is funny, honest, and irresistible. Together they are flirty, sexy and a match made in wine heaven."

–Harlequin Junkie Top Pick

"This will definitely make my list of top reads this year. I can't wait for the next book to see what else is coming."

–Reviews from the Heart

SO RIGHT
So Hot, Book Two

"If the people don't pull you in, the emotions will."
–Hopeless Romantic

"...a great, emotional love story..."
–Romance Book Reviews for You

Historical Romance

The Untouchables Series

THE FORBIDDEN DUKE
"...one can't help but fall in love. This is a wonderful read..."
-Teatime and Books, 5 Stars

THE DUKE OF DARING
"You will not be able to put it down once you start. Such a good read."

-Books Need TLC

THE DUKE of DECEPTION
"...an enjoyable, well-paced story ... Ned and Aquilla are an engaging, well-matched couple – strong, caring and compassionate; and ...it's easy to believe that they will continue to be happy together long after the book is ended."
-All About Romance

THE DUKE of DESIRE
"Masterfully written with great characterization...with a flourish toward characters, secrets, and romance... Must read addition to "The Untouchables" series!"

-My Book Addiction and More

THE DUKE of DEFIANCE
"This story was so beautifully written, and it hooked me from page one. I couldn't put the book down and just had to read it in one sitting even though it meant reading into the wee hours of the morning."

-Buried Under Romance

THE DUKE of DANGER

"Another book hangover by Darcy! Every time I pick a favorite in this series, she tops it. The ending was perfect and made me want more."

-Sassy Book Lover

THE DUKE of ICE

"Each book gets better and better, and this novel was no exception. I think this one may be my fave yet! 5 out 5 for this reader!"

-Front Porch Romance

THE DUKE of RUIN

" ...everything I could ask for in a historical romance... impossible to stop reading."

-The Bookish Sisters

THE DUKE of LIES

"THE DUKE OF LIES is a work of genius! The characters are wonderfully complex, engaging; there is much mystery, and so many, many lies from so many people; I couldn't wait to see it all uncovered."

-Buried Under Romance

THE DUKE of SEDUCTION

"This book was an absolute joy to read. It had all of the things I love about historical-it brought me to another world and completely sucked me in. I couldn't wait for the moments when they were alone and the chemistry between them was undeniable. I always recommend Darcy!"

-Brittany and Elizabeth's Book Boutique

Legendary Rogues Series

LADY of DESIRE

"A fast-paced mixture of adventure and romance, very much in the mould of *Romancing the Stone* or *Indiana Jones*."

-All About Romance

ROMANCING the EARL

"Once again Darcy Burke takes an interesting story and...turns it into magic. An exceptionally well-written book."

-Bodice Rippers, Femme Fatale, and Fantasy

LORD of FORTUNE

"I don't think I know enough superlatives to describe this book! It is wonderfully, magically delicious. It sucked me in from the very first sentence and didn't turn me loose—not even at the end ..."

-Flippin Pages

Secrets & Scandals Series

HER WICKED WAYS

"A bad girl heroine steals both the show and a highwayman's heart in Darcy Burke's deliciously wicked debut."

—Courtney Milan, *NYT* Bestselling Author

HIS WICKED HEART

"Intense and intriguing. Cinderella meets *Fight Club* in a historical romance packed with passion, action and secrets."

—Anna Campbell, *Seven Nights in a Rogue's Bed*

TO SEDUCE A SCOUNDREL

"Darcy Burke pulls no punches with this sexy, romantic page-turner. Sevrin and Philippa's story grabs you from the first scene and doesn't let go. To Seduce a Scoundrel is simply delicious!"

—Tessa Dare, *NYT* Bestselling Author

TO LOVE A THIEF

"With refreshing circumstances surrounding both the hero and the heroine, a nice little mystery, and a touch of heat, this novella was a perfect way to pass the day."

—The Romanceaholic

NEVER LOVE A SCOUNDREL

"I loved the story of these two misfits thumbing their noses at society and finding love." Five stars.

—A Lust for Reading

SCOUNDREL EVER AFTER

"There is something so delicious about a bad boy, no matter what era he is from, and Ethan was definitely delicious."

-A Lust for Reading

About the Author

Darcy Burke is the USA Today Bestselling Author of hot, action-packed historical and sexy, emotional contemporary romance. Darcy wrote her first book at age 11, a happily ever after about a swan addicted to magic and the female swan who loved him, with exceedingly poor illustrations.

A native Oregonian, Darcy lives on the edge of wine country with her guitar-strumming husband, their two hilarious kids who seem to have inherited the writing gene. They're a crazy cat family with two Bengal cats, a small, fame-seeking cat named after a fruit, and an older rescue Maine Coon who is the master of chill and five a.m. serenading. In her "spare" time Darcy is a serial volunteer enrolled in a 12-step program where one learns to say "no," but she keeps having to start over. She's also a fair-weather runner, and her happy places are Disneyland and Labor Day weekend at the Gorge. Visit Darcy online at http://www.darcyburke.com and sign up for her new releases newsletter, follow her on Twitter at http://twitter.com/darcyburke, or like her Facebook page, http://www.facebook.com/darcyburkefans.

CPSIA information can be obtained
at www.ICGtesting.com
Printed in the USA
FFHW021810240219
50614564-56011FF

9 781944 576141